Additional Reviews for *The Key to Me*

The Key to Me is a must read for anyone interested in personal growth. The authors masterfully introduce complex principles in a way that is both thought provoking and yet magically simple. It will enlighten you, touch you, and change your life. I highly recommend this book.

—Mark Victor Hansen, co-author *Chicken Soup for the Soul* series

This book is a testament to Holistic Health, Hypnosis and Complimentary Care. The carefully designed chapters lead the reader on to wanting to learn more and more. Each nugget of truth brings the mind to a place of desiring to go deeper and deeper into the self. You have truly united body, mind, spirit, and emotion in this book. It is sure to be a welcome edition for anyone looking for integration and a better life.

—Anne H. Spencer-Beacham, PhD, founder/president International Medical and Dental Hypnotherapy Assoc., Infinity Institute International, Inc.

An informative and heartfelt way to avoid victimhood and proceed to the joy in your life.

—Larry Moss, acting coach and director

Congratulations on *The Key to Me*! Your efforts will undoubtedly help every person who takes advantage of the insight and wisdom. The organization of the text beginning with mental issues, followed by emotional and physical concerns and concluding with spiritual perspectives is brilliant!

—Dr. Gerard W. Clum, president, Life Chiropractic College West

The Key to Me

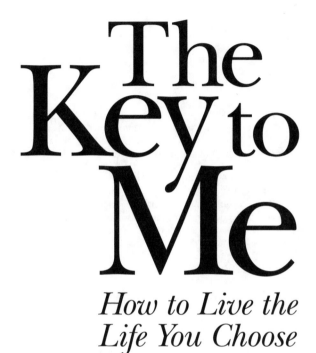

The Key to Me

*How to Live the
Life You Choose*

Cathleen Follansbee, C.Ht.
and Russell LeBlanc, D.C.

SPIDERWEB PUBLISHING
Maple City, MI

Published by Spiderweb Publishing
136 W. Hlavka Road
Maple City, MI 49664
www.LiveTrue.com

Publisher's Cataloging-in-Publication Data
Follansbee, Cathleen.

    The key to me : how to live the life you choose / by Cathleen Follansbee and Russell LeBlanc. –Maple City, MI : Spiderweb, 2003.

    p ; cm.

    Includes bibliographical references
    ISBN 0-9723777-0-0

    1. Self –actualization (Psychology). 2. Self-realization. 3. Success. I. LeBlanc, Russell.
II. Title.

BF637.S4 F65 2003   2002112286
158.1—dc21   0301

Project coordination by Jenkins Group, Inc. • www.bookpublishing.com
Cover design by Ann Pellegrino
Interior design by Barb Hodge

Printed in the United States of America

07 06 05 04 03 * 5 4 3 2 1

Contents

Acknowledgments
Introduction
Section One: The Mental

How the Mind Works 3
Accessing the Subconscious 7
Thought..8
Perceptions, Filters, and Attitudes 10
Reference List 12
    Exercise 1-1: Define your reference list 13
Role of Advertising in Creating Our Filters 14
Self-Talk...14
Words 15
    Exercise 1-2: Removing negativity from your
    speech 17
    Exercise 1-3: Changing your words.....................17
Affirmations..18
    Exercise 1-4: Identifying the filters that limit you.19
    Exercise 1-5: Using affirmations.........................19
Intention...20
    Exercise 1-6: Create with your intentions 22
Meditation...22
    Exercise 1-7: Beginners' meditation 23
Dreams 23
    Exercise 1-8: Problem solving with your dreams...24
Analyzing Dreams 25
Section One Highlights...27

Section Two: The Emotional

Emotion...30
    Exercise 2-1: Feeling emotions 31
Honoring Our Emotions 33

Taking Responsibility 35
Multisensory vs. Five-Sensory.......................36
    Exercise 2-2: Tuning into your other senses 38
Energy as a Barometer 38
Choices 40
Stress 41
Change 42
Detachment..43
    Exercise 2-3: Attachment or detachment?............43
Claiming Our Power 44
Forgiveness...46
    Exercise 2-4: Feeling forgiveness...........................47
Relationships 48
Mirroring..49
    Exercise 2-5: Explore mirroring
    to learn about your life 51
    Exercise 2-6: How do you feel about yourself?......52
    Exercise 2-7: How do you feel about your mate?..53
Communication 53
Communication Type 54
    Find Your Basic Communication Type 55
    Visual..56
    Kinesthetic...57
    Auditory 57
    Digital..58
    Communication Type Summary..........................58
Section Two Highlights 60

Section Three: The Physical

Putting It Together 64
Real vs. Pretend 66
    Exercise 3-1: Remembering a lemon.....................66
The Creation of "Baggage" 68

    Exercise 3-2: Feeling comfort/discomfort..............70
Growth vs. Protection.......................................70
Mind/Body Connections 73
Treatment of the Body 74
Nervous System Function 77
The Physical Body...78
Matter...79
Physical Properties of Matter..........................81
Time and Aging..83
    Exercise 3-3: Your beliefs on aging.......................85
Feeling Challenged 86
Section Three Highlights.................................88

Section Four: The Spiritual

What to Call It?..92
    Exercise 4-1: Feelings about creation....................92
Our Non-Physical Reality: Technology......................92
Our Non-Physical Reality: Spirit..............................94
Religion 95
Stages of Spiritual Growth..............................96
    Exercise 4-2: Am I happy?...................................97
Empowerment and Truth................................97
    Exercise 4-3: Your truth.....................................99
How to Differentiate between Personality and Spirit......99
Manifestation..102
Full Circle..104
    Exercise 4-4: What are your priorities?...............105
Section Four Highlights 106

Afterword...107

Recommended Reading 108

Acknowledgments

A special thanks to Jo Anne Wilson and Michael Camp for their guidance, support, and encouragement.

We wish also to individually thank our families:

Cathy
Thanks, Mom and Dad, for helping me to become the person I am and for loving me no matter what. Brian and Tessa, you are my anchors, my loves, and the best part of my life.

Russ
Mom and Dad, I thank you for always being there and for allowing me to live my life the way I choose. Darlene, Andrew, and Breland, I thank you for all your sacrifices and your continued love and support as I've learned to live my truth. I love you deeply and value you more than anything in my life.

We would also like to take this opportunity to thank a few of the teachers who have brought us to this point in our lives and without whose influence there would be no book. Dr. Deepak Chopra, Bruce H. Lipton, Ph.D., Gary Zukav, Caroline Myss, Dr. Wayne Dyer, Shakti Gawain, and Marianne Williamson have all had a tremendous impact on our lives and our understanding of what life is really all about. To them and countless other of our teachers, a heartfelt "Thank you."

Introduction

This book is about who you really are and how you can make your life better. Underneath the hair, face, clothes, and skin, you share with every other person four aspects of being human. It is by understanding these mental, emotional, physical, and spiritual aspects that you can begin to unlock your potential and live the life you choose.

As you learn about each of the four aspects, you will come to understand their differences but also how they are interconnected. You will learn that the mental aspect is about thought, about how your mind works, about your beliefs, perceptions, and attitudes. The emotional aspect concerns your feelings, the emotions you experience, how they affect your life, and the choices you make. You will learn that each emotion vibrates at a different rate, and therefore each emotion affects the body differently. The physical aspect deals with your physical body and the physical world in which we live and also how the other three aspects affect your physical world. The spiritual aspect concerns your connection to yourself, to the world around you, and to the life force of creation.

This book has had a life of its own. It would not be still. It had to be written. The information follows the format of a popular class series we have taught. Putting this information into written form has allowed us the opportunity not only to cover the information we taught in the classes but also to expand on that information.

In our own personal lives, we have always looked for understanding as to why something happens or why we find ourselves in certain situations. We have looked at the possibility that life is just a random series of unconnected events, but that explanation made us feel like victims with no power to change or be in control of our lives. We finally realized there are basic concepts, principles, and universal laws that govern our lives, and it is how we choose to apply those principles that determines how effective we are at creating the lives we desire. In this book we hope to share this information with you.

Our goal in writing this book was to simplify complicated concepts and bring the flow of information into a format that leads step by step to a greater understanding of life. This greater understanding then leads to more choices. You can ask yourself, "What do I want from my life, and how can I get it?"

We have specifically chosen to bring you a wide variety of information as opposed to going into great depth on a few topics. We have tried to provoke thought and have you ask questions of yourself helping you discover the answers rather than by giving them to you. We encourage you to take this opportunity to find those areas that are of particular interest to you so that you can research them further. Also, take this opportunity to observe where you draw your lines. Just how far are you willing to go to embrace a new concept? If you find yourself doubting some of this information, be aware of what it is and why. This is an opportunity to learn about yourself.

We have purposefully quoted many authors in this book. They are excellent reference sources, and we encourage you to read all the books quoted in this text as well as those on the recommended reading list.

There are many ways to read a book. In reading this one, we recommend that you spend time with each section. First, read through the book in its entirety; then go back through and take a week *living* each section by doing the exercises and working daily with the concepts.

For some of you, this book may bring together concepts you understand individually but have never before connected; for others it may simply remind you of what you already know. For many more, the ideas, questions, and concepts may all be new. To all of you who hold this book…Welcome! Read on! Get to know yourself!

Cathy Follansbee
and
Russ LeBlanc

Section One:

The Mental

"Happiness is when what you think, what you say, and what you do are in harmony."

—Mahatma Gandhi

"Knowledge is proud that he has learned so much; Wisdom is humble that he knows no more."

—Lao Tzu

How the Mind Works

HAVE YOU EVER WONDERED how ordinary people can do such extraordinary things? We have all read about or personally seen heroic deeds. In fact, during recent history we have witnessed many such deeds. On September 11, 2001, during the terrorist attacks on the United States, many people exhibited heroic behavior. We saw firefighters and police officers run into burning and collapsing buildings. We saw co-workers assist and in some cases even carry each other down flight after flight of stairs. We saw a small group of people willing to risk everything to stop a hijacked plane headed for yet more death and destruction.

What makes ordinary people do such extraordinary things? In times of crisis we often forget to ask ourselves what we *can* do and know only what we *must* do. Our minds recognize what must be done and supply our bodies with the fuel they need to accomplish the goal. To gain a clearer understanding of this process, we must first understand how the mind works.

There are three parts to our minds: the conscious, the subconscious, and the unconscious. The conscious mind is the part that is analytical, rational, and judgmental. It is the location of willpower and temporary memory. Our conscious minds begin to develop somewhere around the age of seven and continue to develop over the next several years. At that time, we begin to think in a more adult manner and use logic and reason, and we begin to understand the sequencing of events. Our conscious minds use the filters and perceptions that are housed in our subconscious to analyze situations or problems and to choose appropriate actions.

If you are thinking about making a purchase, anything from a candy bar to a car, it is your conscious mind that shuffles through the information available in the subconscious. To make a decision, it uses logic and takes into account more data than you can imagine, including cost, color, previous experiences, and likes and dislikes. Often it does it in seconds.

The subconscious mind, on the other hand, believes what it is told. Much like the hard drive on a computer, it receives information and files it away. Whatever experiences, sights, smells, sounds, or thoughts enter into the subconscious become fact and remain. The subconscious mind is also the location of permanent memory, emotions, and habits. As children, prior to age seven, we operate primarily out of our subconscious. We live a more carefree and moment-to-moment existence, all the while absorbing information, creating memories, and programming. It is easy to be spontaneous and impulsive. Have you ever watched children play at the beach? Often a child will come running from the water and roll in the sand. The reason for this is quite simply that it *feels good*, it's warm, and it's fun.

**A young child is able to enjoy only
feelings created, with no concerns.**

But at some point in his or her growth, based on previous experiences, a child makes the choice to use a towel. The thought process could go something like this: "Boy, that sand looks warm, but if I get all sandy, I'll have to go back into the water to clean off. My bathing suit will get all sandy, too. I hate that feeling of sand in my bathing suit. My hair will get all sandy. I will look foolish. Besides, it's too close to the time I have to leave, and Mom will get mad if I take too long." On and on it goes. The child is now using his or her conscious mind to make the decision and is putting a new memory into the subconscious—that of using a towel. Typically, from this point on, the child will draw on this new memory. It will become ingrained, and the child will always use a towel. While it is a necessary step in growth to learn how to make choices through the conscious mind, often the capacity for spontaneity is lost or compromised in the process.

Are you an expert at eliminating enjoyment even before it happens?

The unconscious mind is also part of the subconscious. This part of our mind controls our immune system responses and regulates autonomic body functions. When we experience extreme joy or sorrow and tears fill our eyes, it is the unconscious that triggers this physical response. Likewise, when we are frightened by something and our bodies respond with increased heart rates, increased rates of respiration, and muscular contractions, this also is controlled by the unconscious. The unconscious deals in nerve impulses rather than the processes of thought. (We will go into much more detail about this in Section Three.) *Where the conscious mind applies logic and the subconscious stores information in the form of experiences and memories, the unconscious controls how our bodies respond to both the conscious and subconscious.*

The man who carried a coworker down flight after flight of stairs during the terrorist attack of September 11, 2001, did not stop to weigh his decision. He did not dwell on evaluating the pros and cons. He saw what needed to be done to save another human being, picked the person up, and got going. Having stepped out of the conscious mind, his subconscious took over and pulled up the data regarding the danger of the situation and what needed to be done. His unconscious mind then created the body responses and the strength that allowed him to actually carry his coworker all that way. When you think about it, often it is only after a crisis has passed that our conscious minds begin to judge, analyze, and even doubt what has happened as well as our response to the situation.

Throughout each day, we shift through these three parts of our minds continually. *As the result of a circumstance or situation, we have a thought (conscious), the information is received and recorded, which elicits associated emotions (subconscious), and physical responses are triggered in our bodies (unconscious). All of this happens without our even being aware of the process.*

conscious → subconscious → unconscious

Most of us operate primarily out of one part of our mind or the other. The balance is different for each individual. Almost all adults have grown to the point where they have fully developed conscious minds, but we all know people who seem to still operate primarily from their subconscious. Often when choosing a career, we are guided by these tendencies. People are divided into left-brain/conscious mind (technical or masculine) or right-brain/subconscious mind (creative or feminine) thinkers. We will generally be drawn to work with the side that is more dominant.

Left-Brain Tendency	Right-Brain Tendency
Engineers	Artists
Accountants	Actors
Policemen	Inventors
Computer Programmers	Writers

The above list is a generalization to simplify this concept. The goal is to have some type of balance: to be an engineer who is a gourmet cook or an artist who is a whiz with the checkbook.

Accessing the Subconscious

Scientists claim that humans actively use only ten to fifteen percent of their brain capacity. These are the parts that can be measured, the conscious and the unconscious mind. The remaining eighty-five to ninety percent houses a portion of the subconscious mind, which holds knowledge beyond belief. This has the memory of every book we have ever read and every T.V. show or movie we have ever seen. It holds the memories of our whole lives back to the birth process and beyond. Even the greatest computer doesn't have the ability to sort, compare, digest, combine, and bring forth as much information as our subconscious.

Hypnosis is one effective tool that can be used to bypass the conscious mind. With hypnosis it is possible to access our permanent memory and habitual patterns and emotions. A trained hypnotherapist can help us regress deep into our subconscious mind to access this information. Most people can retrieve information as simple as what they were wearing at their fifth birthday party or as complex as the root cause of their claustrophobia. This understanding of the mind has also fostered many other new techniques. Some incorporate guided visualization to fight disease, while others utilize the process of repatterning for habit control. They are all based, in some fashion, on the power of the mind and its healing effects on our bodies. We also naturally access our subconscious minds many times each day. This is called the hypnagogic state. Have you ever driven from point A to point B and realized that you don't remember the past couple of miles? Is there a simple activity such as cutting the grass, typing, or doing the dishes that allows you to just "drift off"? Do you daydream? These are all natural hypnotic states, as is the time just before fully waking and just before falling asleep. These are times when we naturally transcend from the conscious to the subconscious, and they are very powerful.

Thought

We all have brains, nervous systems, and minds that allow us to use thought, to create with thought, and to use the cognitive abilities of our minds for problem solving. These abilities are primarily the conscious mind processes of logic, rationale, analysis, and judgment. These abilities are also why human beings are the most highly evolved species on planet earth.

It seems as though our highly evolved minds and nervous systems function in two capacities: either we create thought or we receive thought. We've all had the experience of using the biological process of thinking to solve a problem or to rationalize a situation to its conclusion. On the other hand, we've all probably also had the experience of an idea popping into our minds seemingly out of nowhere. It's almost as if our brains are able to tap into a vast sea of knowledge and information. Whether we call it intuition, a hunch, or a gut feeling, it is essentially an idea, a thought, or a sense of knowing that did not come through the filter of our conscious minds.

So, is thought something we receive or something we create? Actually, it is a combination of both! Thought precedes everything. Think about it. Every action we take, every word we speak, every invention ever created, and even our attitudes and emotions are first preceded by thought. Take the example of waking to an alarm clock. Before you can even reach over to turn off the alarm, you must first have the thought that it is ringing and that you need to turn it off (or hit the snooze button).

What follows then is a whole series of thought-preceded events. You can look at the clock and groan and think that you have not had enough rest. You can think that you are still tired and that it's going to be a long day. You can drag yourself from bed. Or, you may choose to feel well rested, grateful for another day, and leap out of bed eagerly anticipating the day and the challenges it may bring. Recognize that either way, thoughts have just created the reality that will shape your day.

When you change your thinking, you change your life.

This basic understanding is the foundation of our teaching. Let's look at the previous example again. The action of reaching for the clock, the attitudes associated with your level of rest, your emotional response, and even the words you use (even to yourself) are all preceded by thought.

Thought is at the very foundation of how you create your experiences, and your experiences are your life.

As thinking beings, we create our reality either consciously or unconsciously. Many people live a reactionary life and create their reality and make choices with little or no awareness of the process. Unaware of the power of their thoughts, they seem to lack control of their lives and just let life happen to them. Are you such a person? Do you live at the effect of situations and circumstances? Do you react to what has already happened in your life rather than creating your life the way you desire it to be?

You can actually gain control of your thoughts by using a three-step process. First, you must be aware of what you are thinking and evaluate it. If it is not beneficial to you, you can, second, cancel the thought. Third, you can substitute a different thought. Once you become aware of your thoughts, such as your mental reaction to the alarm clock, you can consciously choose to cancel or eliminate those thoughts and substitute ones that will affect you in a more positive manner. Canceling a thought is no different than pushing the delete key on your computer. You can simply delete the previous thought and substitute a more positive or appropriate one. As you become more aware of the power of your thoughts, you can choose to replace those thoughts that do not enhance your life. Using this simple technique can bring about positive change in your life.

Perceptions, Filters, and Attitudes

As children we operate primarily out of our subconscious. It is through our personal experiences, teachings, and observations that we begin to formulate our belief structures. These beliefs then become the filters through which we see the world. Our filters shape our personalities, create our attitudes, and in general, direct the way we operate in the world.

**Our perceptions of the world and the
circumstances in it are colored by our filters.**

Imagine there are two women walking down the street. The first has the attitude that nothing good ever happens to her. Life never seems to go her way. She is negative, skeptical, and angry.

As she marches down the street, she sees nothing but cement. The second woman is a happy person who sees beauty and loves life. She feels the breeze on her face and the sun on her back. She enjoys the flowers along the way. Which woman do you think will see a hundred-dollar bill lying in the dirt?

Do you see how the filters through which they see the world (happy and positive or angry and negative) attract the situations to them that will reinforce their beliefs? Their perceptions of the world are colored by their filters. Even if she had not found the hundred dollars, the happy woman would still have had a positive experience as she walked down the street because she had a positive attitude. She perceived the world as a happy place. The unhappy woman had a negative experience because she had a negative attitude. She perceived the world as a gloomy, even angry, place. When you are in this state, you don't attract wonderful things to yourself. It's as if you look through tinted glass that colors your world. The tint in the glass is made up of your filters. *You have an experience. It creates a perception (belief). This belief then creates an attitude.*

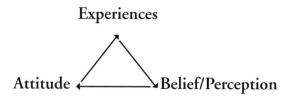

Experiences

Attitude ← → **Belief/Perception**

Your attitude can then create, or attract to you, another similar experience. In other words, a happy person will generally continue to attract happy experiences. An angry person will generally continue to attract experiences that will reinforce the anger. Your filters will always influence the way you perceive your world and will continue to operate throughout your life. If you have a gloomy attitude, you have filters in place that will reinforce that attitude for you. Chances are that if you have a negative outlook, you will see a glass that is half empty rather than half full every time you look at a glass with only half of what it can hold. Determining your filters is a good place to start looking at how you can change your life. By changing your filters, you can change your life.

Reference List

Have you ever noticed how your attention is captured when you hear your name spoken or the name of your hometown? Have you ever bought a new jacket or even a new car with great excitement only to begin to see one on every corner? Someone you know may even have the same jacket, and you wonder why you never noticed it before. You were unaware of the jacket because, prior to your purchase, it had no relevance to you.

Your mind contains your own personally relevant reference list of information. This reference list is the byproduct of your beliefs, experiences, interactions, observations, and attitudes. It not only affects the quality of your everyday life but also dictates those experiences to which you are likely to be attracted. In other words, this reference list reflects your filters, and it is through your filters that you look out into the world. The following are a few examples of items that are found on personal reference lists:

Personal Reference List
- Your name/family name
- Colors you like/don't like

- Religious/political/racial/social affiliations
- Cars you have owned
- Places you have lived, visited, or wish to visit
- Fears (spiders, snakes, flying, etc.)
- Skills/education you have or desire to have
- People or characteristics you admire or identify with
- Money
- Clothing

For most people the list is lengthy. Plus, you continually add to your reference list by having new experiences. Purchasing that new jacket or car adds that item to your reference list. If you move to an area that experiences earth tremors or quakes, then earthquakes will be added to your reference list.

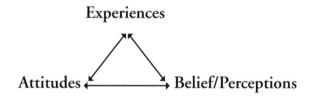

Experiences

Attitudes ⟷ **Belief/Perceptions**

Exercise 1-1: Define your reference list

Make a personal reference list. List things that you notice when you come across them. Use the above list as an example.

Review the list. Does it help you determine what type of person you are? Are you positive or negative?

Look at opportunities or positive experiences you may have missed in your life. Look at why. Were you too focused on possible negative drawbacks or outcomes?

Role of Advertising in Creating Our Filters

The advertising industry is a powerful force behind creating filters. A good advertising campaign doesn't just sell a product; it sells an image. The purpose is to make us see the image in the ad and to identify with it. For instance, if you see people who are happy, healthy, thin, beautiful, and fulfilled, do you want to be like them? Do you want to have what they have? Whether or not you are even thinking about the product, if you believe or let in the perception that this is how a person should look, you now have a new filter. You will measure yourself and everyone else by this filter from now on. Ads create product demand partially through creating filters, but once you have the filter in place, it is yours. This is a good example of the concept that whatever your subconscious is told, it believes!

Self-Talk

Are you aware of the little voice, that inner critic, that plays inside your head all the time? It's that little voice that narrates, judges, compares, and dictates what you experience in life. It's your self-talk. One of the best ways to be aware of your perceptions, filters, and attitudes is to listen to your self-talk. When faced with an important test or challenge, is your self-talk telling you that you are confident and prepared to handle the challenge, or does it fill you with doubt and tell you that you are not prepared and are going to fail? When you see yourself naked in the mirror, what does that voice have to say? Does that voice tell you that you are beautiful and reinforce how you love and accept yourself, or does that voice tell you that you are fat, unattractive, and imperfect? Learning to really hear what you say to yourself will give you insight about your filters and attitudes.

Words

An awareness of the words we speak is another tool to help us understand our perceptions, filters, and attitudes. Listen to your words; they tell you (and others) how you think.

While your self-talk reflects thoughts that are not expressed outwardly, the words you speak are the thoughts that you share with the world. Words are really thoughts expressed in form. They are your thoughts in action. They tell the world who you are and what beliefs, perceptions, filters, and attitudes you hold.

You demonstrate your thoughts through your words.

When you listen, what do you hear yourself say? Do you say things like, "I'm not good at math" or "I can't run fast" or "I don't like vegetables"? Look at the limitations you put on yourself. On the other hand, positive words speak of the positive attitudes and beliefs you hold.

Words used and heard repeatedly reinforce and shape perceptions, filters, attitudes, and even experiences. For instance, the first word many children learn is "no." This word by its very nature can stop them (as is generally the intention), but it may also restrict them from further exploration and may even shut down that creative and adventuresome nature that is natural for a child. Think about how often a child is exploring the world and gets near something of value, something that can be harmful, or something the child can damage. It could be the television, a candle, a plant, bookshelf, or just about anything. At this point, usually some well-meaning adult firmly tells the child, "no." This scenario is repeated over and over for a child. While it does teach children not to touch, when it happens continually, it may also dampen their sense of wonder. They may become less adventuresome. This is certainly easier for the adult, but it restricts one of the main avenues of learning and creativity for children. These effects can be long lasting.

Discovery and adventure are necessary aspects of children's growth and development. They play an integral part in setting their perceptions, filters, and attitudes and in shaping the type of people they will become. As an adult, how many times have you rejected an opportunity simply because you were responding to the doubt and negativity learned as a child? How many adventures, challenges, or risks have you turned away from simply because of this programming? It is sad to think that this place of "safety" you may have learned as a child could become more comfortable to you than the natural state of creativity that is, in fact, your birthright. "No" and "not" are two very overused words in our language. In fact, try to eliminate them from your vocabulary and you will realize just how often you use them.

Negative thoughts and words can limit how life is experienced. When you eliminate the negativity and the "would have," "could have," "should have" phrases from your life, you open yourself to living life more fully. The list below gives examples of commonly used phrases that represent the limitations and negativity so often seen in the world:

Stop Using	Start Using
I can't (couldn't)	I can
I won't	I will
I doubt that	I am sure that
I fear that	I am confident that
Nothing will	Everything will
I'm uncertain	I am certain
I'm unable	I am able
I should	I could or I will
I don't know	I know

Exercise 1-2: Removing negativity from your speech

Take just one day and monitor your thoughts and verbal expressions in an attempt to eliminate or cut down on the use of the words "no" and "not" in your speech. Try to be aware of each time you use these words and substitute a positive word in its place. When someone asks you to do something that is unappealing to you, rather than answer with a "no" response, try "I think I'll pass this time." If your child asks you to do something for him or her that you know could be done for themself, rather than say "no," try saying, "I'd like you to do that for yourself."

This is an important exercise. Try it and try to stick with it. See how you have done at the end of the day. Sometimes it takes a little thought to come up with an alternative reply, but it gets easier. You may just be out of practice.

The word "no" is just too easy to use.

The three-step process on page 10 for controlling our thoughts certainly applies when reprogramming our vocabulary. You may wish to review these steps.

Exercise 1-3: Changing your words

Wear a rubber band loosely around your wrist. Each time you become aware you are using a word or phrase you wish to eliminate, snap the rubber band to interrupt the thought process. Say or think "cancel" or "delete" and substitute a more appropriate word or phrase. This really works; try it!

Affirmations

Webster's College Dictionary defines affirmations as "positive declarations." We view them much the same way as self-talk—they can be positive or negative. You can affirm either positive thoughts and attitudes or negative thoughts and attitudes. Charles Ward, motivational speaker, once said, "If you talked to anyone else the way you talk to yourself, they would never speak to you again." How true! The self-talk you use with yourself is a form of affirmation. You hear what you are saying to yourself.

Stop and think whether what you are saying is what you really want to tell yourself.

Your conscious mind observes and evaluates. It is logical and rational. It receives its information from your experiences and thoughts and from those who influence you—your parents, friends, teachers, and even the media. It is influenced by your filters and enters your subconscious mind, that part of your mind that believes whatever it is told.

You move thoughts from your conscious to your subconscious in two primary ways: repetition and/or emotion. You have a thought; you habitually think it; it becomes a belief. Let's say the thought is "I'm no good at math." You heard it repeatedly as a child, and you say it to yourself even now. This thought has become a filter through which you perceive your world. It is on your reference list, something you simply believe to be true: "Math = no good." Do you see how limiting this is? You will never allow yourself to be any better at math (or anything else) until you believe that you can be and that you will be. To change a habit, pattern, or filter, you must first change your thoughts, words, and beliefs.

Exercise 1-4: Identifying the filters that limit you

Take a few minutes to examine your filters. What beliefs or perceptions do you hold about yourself that are limiting your potential? What about your loved ones? Are there beliefs you hold about them that are limiting them?

This is where the power of affirmations applies. The scientific law of neutrality states that if you take a negative charge and add an equally positive charge to it, the charges become neutralized. Likewise, if you have a negative thought and add a positive thought, it can become neutralized. If you keep affirming this new positive thought, you can create a new belief pattern. (This is much the same as the process you learned on canceling a thought and substituting a positive one in its place.)

To use affirmations, follow these three important guidelines:

- Always state in the positive.
- Always state in the present tense.
- Keep it simple.

"I am good at math" is a well-stated affirmation. It is simple, positive, and in the present tense.

Exercise 1-5: Using affirmations

Write your affirmations on sticky notes and post them in places where you will see them regularly. Each time you see your affirmation, take the time to say it, out loud preferably, but at least to yourself.

Say your affirmations to yourself just before waking fully and just prior to sleep, which is a natural hypnotic state. You are accessing your subconscious directly at these times, and it is highly effective.

Say your affirmations to yourself in the mirror. This is a great way to recognize any barriers or emotional baggage you carry that can keep you from achieving the desired change. Mirror work, really looking yourself in the eyes and focusing on yourself, is a powerful reinforcing mechanism.

It's important to note here that while the use of affirmations on many beliefs and perceptions can be very effective, the use of affirmations alone will not solve or eliminate deep-seated emotional issues such as abuse, abandonment, or relationship issues. When coupled with the appropriate healing therapies, however, they may prove extremely beneficial.

Intention

Intention is one of the single most important concepts to understand. It is the power of directed thought. Intentions are thoughts that crystallize when we focus on something we desire and choose to let it dictate our priorities and/or direction. Our thoughts create our intentions, and our intentions dictate the actions taken to reach our goals or fulfill our desires.

Intentions set processes in motion that affect every aspect of our lives. They create our experiences and the changes we desire in our lives. Intention is of the future. What we give our attention to is in the present. *As long as we focus our attention on our intention, we will create what we intend.* The ability to recognize where we place our attention will allow us to see whether we are indeed supporting our intention.

For instance, if your intention is to have a better, more loving relationship with your family and it just isn't happening, stop and look at where you are putting your attention. Are you spending all your time at work? With friends? Pursuing a hobby? Remember to keep your focus on the present. If change is needed, do it now. Now, in each present moment, is where your future is created.

You create your reality with thoughts, fueled by intention.

Gary Zukav, in his book *Seat of the Soul,* states: "The decisions that you make and the actions that you take upon the earth are the means by which you evolve. At each moment you choose the intentions that will shape your experiences and those upon which you will focus your attention."

Conflicting intentions occur when you have two different intentions that are opposed to each other. This often happens when it comes to creating change. For instance, perhaps part of you really wants to move to another city and fully intends to move. However, you also desire or intend to remain close to your family. In this situation the strongest intention will win and manifest itself in your life. If neither is stronger, you may just stay in a state of struggle. Attitudes also reflect intentions. For example, say you have the attitude that you are better than others or that some races truly are superior. With this attitude, will you have a difficult time creating an intention to see the beauty in all life and to come from a place of unconditional love? When you experience conflicting intentions, you are generally looking through your filters. This is an opportunity for true growth and healing to take place. Be willing to identify the filters that are being shown to you and choose whether they serve your highest good.

Remember this: *your intentions and where you place your attention are at this very moment creating your future.* You can act automatically, or you can choose to become more aware, more conscious, of the choices you are making. What really are your intentions?

Exercise 1-6: Create with your intentions

Pick an area in your life where you are experiencing struggle. Identify what you want, how you truly desire it to be.
Now look at your actions. Look at where you are putting
your attention. Does it support your intention? What do
you need to do to change? Look at short-term actions and
long-term goals. Write them down and commit to them.
Follow your plan of action and keep your attention
focused on your intention.

Meditation

The concept of meditation can seem contrary to the power
of intention and directed thought. It is about not thinking and
not focusing one's thoughts. One of the purposes of meditation
is to transcend the conscious mind in order to access the power
of the subconscious. This allows us to enjoy the natural state of
being rather than *doing*. Meditation is, in fact, a natural process
and can be reached simply by being still long enough for the
chatterbox conscious mind to quiet itself. Sometimes the greatest difficulty is to discipline ourselves to take the time to be still
in order to allow transcendence to occur. Meditation is an
effortless process that can bring about higher awareness, greater
appreciation, stress reduction, and improved sleep patterns. It
brings us into the present moment. It is counterproductive to
resist this natural process by trying to control our thoughts.

The effects of meditation are so extensive that we encourage you to take time out for yourself each day to experience
its many benefits. There are many kinds of meditation and
many techniques that can be utilized in order to reach this
state. You will experience a simple meditation in Exercise 1-7

below. You may also wish to explore more fully a variety of meditation techniques.

Exercise 1-7: Beginners' meditation

Find a quiet comfortable place to be seated. Close your eyes and bring the focus of your attention inward to your breath. Allow your thoughts to simply flow across the screen of your mind. Resist nothing; judge nothing. If thoughts distract you, merely bring your focus back to your breathing. Allow your breathing to carry you into a quiet, still state of being.

The average meditation lasts fifteen to thirty minutes, at which time you will naturally return to your conscious, waking state.

Dreams

Dreams are like doors to our subconscious. In fact, dreams are one of the ways the subconscious mind communicates. There are many kinds of dreams. One common type replays the last thought you had before sleep. It may incorporate the movie you just watched or the book you were reading. We also have dreams that teach by giving us insights, valuable lessons, and information. There are also precognitive dreams that contain foreknowing about incidents that have yet to happen in our linear time frame.

The bulk of our nights are spent in slow-wave sleep. Slow-wave sleep has four stages. The first is the earliest phase of sleep, and the fourth is the deepest. During the fourth phase, the brain waves are the slowest; it is the hardest to awaken from these. Our most vivid dreams happen during the rapid eye movement (REM) phase of sleep. REM sleep occurs at approximately ninety-minute intervals, four to five times a night, between peri-ods of slow-wave sleep. Each REM phase becomes longer and more intense. The first REM phase is about fifteen minutes in length, and the final phase lasts up to forty-five minutes. This last occurrence of REM sleep often happens during the final hour of sleep, just before waking. Dreams occurring during this final phase of REM are often the more significant teaching or problem-solving dreams.

Another interesting aspect of dream life is that it is cyclic. In the more external times of spring and summer, dreams are often more difficult to remember. By contrast, in the fall and winter months, typically a more internal, contemplative time, dreams are the clearest and strongest. Also, for women, the time around menses creates strong dreams. Likewise, during the full moon, anyone can experience very strong dreams.

Few people remember their dreams upon waking. Many more remember small fragments but not the whole dream. Most of us can, however, reprogram ourselves to remember our dreams. Try this: place paper and pen or a tape recorder next to your bed. Before lying down to go to sleep, state your intention, out loud or to yourself, to remember your dreams. At any point that you awaken in the night, or first thing in the morning, begin to write down what you remember. It may be as little as a few words or a single sentence, but write it down. As you write, an amazing thing usually happens. More and more pieces of the dream will come to you. Continue to write until you have as complete a description as you are able to receive. As you repeat this process night after night, it becomes easier to remember more of your dream content right at waking.

Exercise 1-8: Problem solving with your dreams

To use your dream time for problem solving, try this: Sit

on the edge of your bed, state your intention to remember your dreams, take a deep breath, and relax. Bring to mind a problem you need insight into or would like to solve. Stay calm. Becoming emotional at this time can keep you awake and interfere with your dreams. State the intention that you are open to receiving a solution or any information that will help you resolve this situation. State also that you would like it to come to you in a way that is easy for you to understand. Let go and climb into bed. Relax and fall asleep. Write or record your dream upon waking. Then use the following method to help you understand your dream.

Analyzing Dreams

There are a multitude of ways to analyze your dreams. After studying several of these methods, we have developed our favorites. Used as a process or flow, our method goes like this:

First, be aware of the feelings and emotions you experience upon waking. Are you happy, sad, frightened, etc.?

Second, see whether you can extract the overall message of the dream. Was there a theme, or does some meaning come to you?

Last, if necessary, look at the individual symbols. In other words, what does "tree" mean to you, what does "home" mean, etc.? There are many books you can purchase to help you with definitions for dream symbols. A good one is *The Dream Book* by Betty Bethards. As you look your symbols up in a book, your purpose is to see whether that definition "feels" right *to you*. This is *your* dream and these are *your* symbols; you have the correct or true definition for *you*. Many times you will agree with the given definition, but for those times when you don't, reading someone else's definition may lead you to your own definition or meaning.

Dream analysis can be both enlightening and entertaining, and you can use your dreams as powerful tools for growth and healing. Everything you know is in your subconscious mind. Your subconscious gives you dreams that have relevance to you and that are a tool you can easily begin to use. Any tool that allows you access to your subconscious mind facilitates great potential for personal growth.

Section One Highlights:

- There are three parts to our minds: the conscious, sub-conscious, and unconscious.
- The conscious is analytical and logical.
- The subconscious believes what it is told and houses all memory.
- The unconscious is responsible for immune system responses and autonomic body functions.
- Thought precedes everything. It is the very foundation of how we create our experiences.
- In our minds is a reference list that reflects our filters and what we perceive in our world.
- Be aware of your attitudes by listening to your self-talk.
- Words are thought in verbal form. They tell you and others how and what you think.
- Affirmations are a tool for reprogramming our thoughts.
- Intentions fuel our desires.
- Meditation allows us to transcend the conscious mind and tap into the subconscious.
- Dreams are like doors to our subconscious.

Section Two:

The Emotional

"*That the birds of worry and care fly above your head, this you cannot change. But that they build nests in your hair, this you can prevent.*"

—Chinese Proverb

"*When we forgive someone, the knots are untied and the past is released.*"

—Reshad Feild

Emotion

When compiling the material for this section, we were surprised to find just how broad a field of information the aspect of emotion covered. Not only does it include individual emotions but also feelings, vibrational energy, and associated concepts such as stress, worry, forgiveness, and even relationships.

Everything is energy vibrating at different rates or speeds. Our perception of something as solid is only that, a perception. Something solid appears solid only because its molecules are vibrating at a slower rate than something that appears as liquid or gas. Energy vibrates at a rate that is slow, fast, or somewhere in between. This is its vibrational frequency. We will expand on these concepts in Section Three, but for now just remember this basic understanding of energy.

Emotions are commonly thought of as feelings, but they have a narrower definition than that. Our emotions are currents of energy, each vibrating at a different rate. What we consider to be negative emotions such as fear, anger, and hatred cause our bodies to feel heavy, dull, and dragged down because they have a lower or slower vibrational frequency. More positive emotions such as love, joy, and gratitude make us feel light and buoyant because they have a higher or faster vibrational frequency.

Emotions, like words, are preceded by thought. First, we have a thought that may create within us an emotion. The emotion then affects that thought by giving it greater energy, which leads to the thought becoming stronger and more powerful. The thoughts that have the greatest impact on us are infused with energy. Our feelings about the death of a loved one or the birth of a child are examples of high energy, emotional thoughts. An unimportant thought such as the color of a doorknob has very little meaning and no emotion attached.

Therefore, it carries virtually no energetic charge.

When we accept the concept that each emotion carries a different vibratory rate, we can then become open to the idea of choosing emotions with higher frequencies. Likewise, when we understand that our thoughts are fueled by our emotions, we will want to choose more positive thoughts, which will link us to more positive emotions that bring with them a higher degree of energy. This higher energy will lift us up and we can then begin the process of mental and emotional healing.

It is important to look at the way the words "emotion" and "feeling" are used. There is a tendency to use them interchangeably, but they are different. Emotions have chemistry; they have vibrational frequencies. Pure emotion separated from thought is basically energy. Feelings have a much broader interpretation. Feelings include instincts, hunches, intuitions, and gut reactions. They also are influenced by thoughts we receive, thoughts we create, associated emotions, and the way our bodies physically experience these thoughts and emotions. There will be more about this in Section Three, under Comfort and Discomfort.

**Emotions, thoughts, and body sensations
combine to create our "feelings."**

Exercise 2-1: Feeling emotions

Find a quiet place where you can be alone and can rest in a comfortable position. Close your eyes and tune into the sensations in your body, such as where you feel relaxed and where you feel tension. Are parts of your body tighter and more contracted than others? Notice your heart rate and breathing. Don't judge or criticize what you are experiencing; just be aware of your physical body.

Now think about something you have experienced that affected you negatively. It may be an argument with someone or something you fear. Let yourself feel this experience and the emotions associated with it. Once you feel yourself involved and experiencing the emotions, shift your awareness to your body. How has your body changed? What physical sensations are you now experiencing? Where in your body do you feel these negative thoughts and emotions? Again, do not judge; just observe.

Take several long, deep breaths and consciously release the thoughts and bring your body back into a more relaxed state. Take deep breaths until you feel your body relax and your heart rate return to normal. Now think about something that is very pleasurable and brings you joy. Perhaps you will think of someone you love and who loves you or an experience in which you felt tremendous joy, love, and happiness or the calming beauty in nature. Entertain these thoughts and emotions for a few moments; enjoy the pleasure in them. Now, once again shift your awareness to your body. How does your body feel now? Is it more relaxed and comfortable?

This exercise illustrates how the energy of thoughts and emotions affects your physical body. *You have a thought (conscious) → emotion is created (subconscious) → your body responds accordingly (unconscious).*

conscious → subconscious → unconscious

Honoring Our Emotions

It is important to realize the value of honoring the emotions we feel at the moment we feel them. It is not just about being aware of our emotions and choosing higher vibrational emotions; that is only part of the process. It is about identifying and accepting what we feel rather than denying or repressing the feelings. We can then let go and move on. Learning this process will allow us to reach a point where we can live in these higher frequencies.

There are really no "good" or "bad" emotions.

It is our judgment of emotions that labels them this way. *Emotions just are.* Likewise, to experience pure emotion is neither a "good" nor "bad" experience. It is when we label an emotion that we become attached to it. If the emotion affects us negatively when internalized, it can become stronger and more harmful. It is important to avoid the tendency to deny, repress, and internalize emotions and feelings. The key is to honestly honor how we are feeling in each moment. In Western society it is very common for people to greet each other by saying, "Hi, how are you?" Unfortunately, this is often an automatic and insincere question. Most people do not really think about how the other person is feeling, nor do they wish to share how they themselves are feeling. Americans are generally rather self-contained. They show the world one face while holding their true feelings inside. By contrast, in some countries and cultures the expressing and sharing of emotions is not only acceptable but also encouraged. There are generalizations we are familiar with, such as the Irish are quick to laugh and quick to temper, Italians are tempestuous, and Latinos are passionate. Israel even has a wailing wall where people can openly express their grief and pain. So the next time you start to answer this greeting by saying,

"Fine, how are you?" stop and think about how you really are feeling. Whether you share the information or not is up to you.

Our *emotions* are preceded by our *thoughts*.
How we *express* them is our *process*.

When we look at emotion as energy, we can gain further understanding of just how damaging the practices of denying, internalizing, and repressing our emotions really are. Remember, emotions are energy and have different vibrational frequencies. Those emotions that are uplifting such as love and joy have a much healthier effect on our beings than do more negative emotions such as anger or fear.

Most of us are familiar with the body's "fight or flight" modes. This is where the body responds to fear and danger by gearing up to respond by fighting or by fleeing. What we are learning now is that all emotions affect our physical bodies. Changes in the body can occur even long after a person has experienced an event that was highly emotional. Muscle tension, depth and rate of breathing, skin sensitivity, and even changes in heart rate may occur in response to thought and emotion. These body changes can actually be measured by a polygraph machine to determine whether a person is lying or telling the truth. Most of the time these changes occur automatically without our awareness.

A common practice in times of crisis and heavy emotion such as anger or fear is to shorten, or even hold, our breath. It's as if we think we can keep the bad feelings out when really all we are doing is holding them in and maybe even adding to them. Over time this can contribute to or cause disease and illness. It has been shown repeatedly that extended periods of stress create many ill effects in the body.

Taking Responsibility

Another important aspect of honoring emotions is taking responsibility for them. We must recognize that these emotions are ours, created within us. It is a healthier response to say, "I feel angry" than to say, "You made me angry." Acknowledging responsibility for one's thoughts and feelings is to honor them without feeling guilt or assigning blame. An important byproduct of this understanding can be improved communication. When we are blaming others, accusing them of creating our feelings, this sends out negative energy. It is generally received and acknowledged in one of two ways: either with retaliatory anger or with defensiveness. In return, people will generally either yell and blame or withdraw and "put up a wall." Either way, by being unaware that we are making a choice not to take responsibility for our feelings, we may have blocked the opportunity for true communication. On the other hand, owning our thoughts and feelings but choosing to share them can lead to more effective communication and greater intimacy.

The mere understanding of these principles doesn't automatically make them work. We must first be clear of much of our emotional baggage. *It is the repressed, internalized, and unresolved emotions and feelings we have that make up our emotional baggage.* It is our unhealed wounds that haunt us.

Many people have past and present emotional issues that need to be addressed and resolved before they can become truly emotionally healthy and stable. Until these wounds have been healed, they may often find themselves in a state of reaction. This happens when we feel our thoughts and emotions happening to us, triggered by people and circumstances outside of ourselves. When we hold onto emotions and emotional baggage in our bodies, it's like wearing a coat covered with buttons.

When these buttons get "pushed," we react.

Think about the last time you overreacted to a situation. Often a seemingly insignificant incident can become a major upset. As an example, say you have repressed a lot of anger in your life. When something happens that would normally be mildly annoying to someone else, in you it triggers all the old, hidden anger and causes you to react out of proportion to the small incident. A good example of this is road rage. Rarely, if ever, is the cause of this extreme anger that someone was cut off in traffic or was being tailgaited. It goes far deeper than that, and it can be this way with many different emotions.

Betrayal can be another big button. In just living our lives, as well as in every relationship, there is an element of trust involved. If you have ever had your trust betrayed, you can understand how deeply this can wound. For many people this is a lifetime pattern that happens over and over. A parent may leave home, friends turn against you, a partner may have an affair, or an employee may steal from you. From childhood friendships to adult relationships and everywhere in between, we put ourselves in the position where we can be hurt and betrayed. If you have issues with betrayal, something that would normally be a minor disappointment such as being stood up for lunch can become huge. Again, you may overreact!

Stop here to take a minute and look inward. Reflect on times when your response has been disproportionate to an incident. How many buttons do you have on your coat?

Multisensory vs. Five-Sensory

In many societies, people become immersed in the physical aspects of being human and surviving in a physical world. People rely very heavily on their five senses to receive information and experience the physical world around them. However, beyond the limitations of the five senses of sight, hearing, taste, smell, and touch, there is a more expanded realm of perception. This expanded realm involves an awareness that we have the ability to perceive our world through more subtle means. In his book *Seat of the Soul*, Gary Zukav refers to this phenomena as "multisensory."

Whether we realize it or not, we are able to sense things that we cannot perceive through our five senses. Have you ever been feeling great and then walked into a room where an argument or crisis had just occurred or was occurring? Do you recall sensing the heaviness and intensity in the room? That awareness was not filtered through your five senses but was, in fact, received through a more subtle means of perception. In *Seat of the Soul* Zukav states "As a personality becomes multisensory, its intuitions—its hunches and subtle feelings—become important to it. It senses things about itself, other people, and the situations in which it finds itself that it cannot justify on the basis of the information that its five senses (alone) can provide."

Focusing on our own personal healing, opening up and releasing our old wounds and their energetic blocks, can clear the way for our multisensory capabilities. With less of the dense, low-frequency energy getting in the way, we are better able to "receive" information. This is the point at which we can begin to look outward toward others. It becomes possible to see their wounds and to be able to see through most of their actions to their true intentions. We are then able to be more compassionate and understanding. Much of this process is done with multisensory awareness.

**There is more to life than birth and death,
with struggle in between.**

We are not here simply to exist! We are here to evolve beyond the physical limitations of this world and to accept a more expanded view, one that goes beyond our physical existence. There is purpose in our lives, there are reasons why we have certain experiences, and there are lessons to be learned from these experiences. Once we recognize that life is not just about the struggle to survive, we can begin to appreciate the broader picture and subtle implications of our experiences. As we evolve beyond our own individual needs to survive and heal, we will begin to recognize our greater connections with others and the broader effects of our choices and actions. We are not alone in this world. Our journey is supported in ways that are only just beginning to be understood.

Begin to get acquainted with your multisensory self! Question the physical evidence that is reported by your five senses! Be aware of your subtle feelings, hunches, and intuitions as they occur and acknowledge, or better yet, act upon them! There is magic that awaits you as you open up to the many possibilities available to you on this journey called life.

Exercise 2-2: Tuning into your other senses

Begin to use your multisensory perceptions. Pause before answering the telephone to receive, to sense, who is calling. Think of someone and send him or her the message to call you. Be aware of coincidences. Look a little deeper at where solutions and answers come from. Start trusting your knowingness and begin to act upon that knowledge.

Energy as a Barometer

As discussed earlier, emotion is really energy vibrating at different frequencies. In fact, everything is energy. (The focus here is on living things. The energy in nonliving things and the concepts about physical matter will be addressed in Section Three.) All living things emit energy. By the very nature of being alive, living things vibrate with life. Scientific technology exists in the form of Kirlian photography to capture the image of energy fields around all living things. In humans, thoughts, emotions, and the vibrational frequency associated with them constantly influence these energy fields. Awareness of how our energy feels and how it is influenced by other people and situations is part of the expanded perception that makes us multisensory.

Think back to the previous example of walking into a room after an argument or crisis. The multisensory feeling was a sensing of the energy in the room. Because the vibratory energy was incompatible with your own, you sensed a feeling of discomfort. That discomfort would be no different than if you were in a bad mood or depressed state and walked into a lively party. We sense energy that is inconsistent with our own. When we sense energy that is incompatible with our own, the feeling we get is one of discomfort. On the other hand, when we experience an energy frequency that is compatible with our own, we sense a feeling of comfort.

As you become more familiar with this awareness of incompatible energy and your associated feelings of comfort and discomfort, you will begin to make choices based on these feelings. You may find yourself avoiding circumstances that do not feel right based upon a strong feeling of discomfort. Likewise, you may find yourself drawn to a situation simply because you feel a strong attraction to it. These multisensory feelings of comfort and discomfort are good indicators of the most appropriate direction for you to take.

Going even further, your home environment and even the clothing you wear are a reflection of who you are and your energetic vibratory rate. Putting money matters aside, your decision to purchase a particular item, be it clothing, furniture, or a car, is often based on how that item makes you feel. What you are sensing, in a multisensory capacity, is how the energy of that item feels when combined with your own. If it feels good, you may buy it. If it does not, you will probably put it back. The tendency is to be attracted to those items that resonate with energy that is compatible with your own. Colors, for instance, have their own vibratory rate. As you make your choices, it's possible you may be sensing something as subtle as the energy of the color when combined with your own.

The ability to sense energy truly is amazing. As you clear your own body energy by healing your wounds, you will become ever more sensitive to the energy all around you. Become more aware of how the energy of your experiences feels to you and give those feelings value by measuring them on a scale of comfort or discomfort.

Choices

By now you can see how the concepts of energy, vibration, and multisensory perceptions apply in your life. Something as simple as the choices you make can be looked at with a new perspective. When you are faced with an important decision, do you still logically weigh the pros and cons, or do you begin to see the value of also checking in with your sense of how it feels to determine what is most appropriate for you? Are you beginning to see how your choices impact not only yourself but also those around you? Is the impact generally much broader than you had realized?

It is at this point that you become more responsible for your choices. The best thing you can do for yourself (and everyone else) is to honor yourself while remaining respectful and loving of others. The most responsible choice may be what best serves you (not your ego, but the highest part of yourself), as long as that doesn't happen at the expense of those around you. This way the choices you make also best serve others. When you shift your priority toward your own personal growth and begin to feel the changes, you become aware that the more you take care of yourself, raise your own vibrations, and begin to truly work for your own higher good, the more you have to offer others.

Stress

Stress is a good example of how our frequencies, or energy, are affected by our thoughts and emotions. Stress, in its simplest definition, is the mental and emotional response to circumstances and situations. In *Scholastic Children's Dictionary*, one of the definitions of stress is, "to make something important," as in, "to stress" it, like, "I stress good nutrition." When you get right down to it, isn't that what we do? We make something important and become attached to it in some way. From that point, our thoughts and emotions reflect that attachment. Then, when things don't go along the predetermined path, we become "stressed out."

> **It's not really what other people think, say, or do,
> and it's not really our circumstances or situations,
> but rather it's how we respond to them that
> creates the stress in our lives.**

It's about what we think, say, and do. The way we respond is a choice we make. Look again at your body's barometer: it's *your* discomfort that creates stress. When you recognize and respect yourself as a being of energy and realize the effects of lower frequency emotions, you begin to realize just how harmful and damaging stress can be. It becomes easier to make choices that do not bring discomfort and create stress.

Change

**Everything in the process of growth and evolution
is in a constant state of change.**

Change is inevitable. Yet, we humans have a tendency to resist it. We fear change. To compensate for this, we tend to develop "comfort zones." These comfort zones are routine, relatively consistent, and predictable. Therefore, they are comfortable. Since the general tendency is to avoid change and it cannot truly be avoided, people often become "out of balance" or stressed when change occurs. How much easier and stress free would our lives be if we learned to simply accept the basic premise that everything is continually changing?

**One certainty that exists in life is the uncertainty
of change. Learn to develop acceptance of the
things you cannot change.**

When we shift our attention to the future or focus on the past, we come face to face with the concept of change. This often brings up the emotions of worry and guilt. Whereas guilt is more often associated with the past, worry is always about the future.

The stress of resisting change and the actual fear of change contribute to the creation of the emotion "worry." Worry is uncertainty, concern, and anxiety about a future that has yet to happen. Worry puts us into a lower frequency vibration and can have far-reaching effects. How we live each present moment creates our future. When we attach worry to the present moment, not only do we negatively impact our present moment, but we also impact our potential future.

The same concept applies when we think about our attachments to things that have occurred in the past. Most of the guilt we experience is our emotional attachment to, and regrets about, experiences that have already occurred that we are powerless in the present to change. By bringing the negativity of past events or experiences into our present, we are affecting our future.

We are creating our future in this moment.
If we bring our past into the present moment,
we are creating a future just like our past.

To live effectively, we must live in the present moment, neither stuck in the past nor worrying about the future. In this state we continue to evolve and flow with the process of change that is inevitably going to take place. If we are living in the present moment, change is not really even recognized; it just is. Life flows, and we flow with it.

Detachment

Whereas acceptance allows the existence of "things you cannot change," detachment is letting go of the things that are not relevant to the present moment. This means letting go of attachment to outcomes and expectations. Consequently, you choose your actions and behaviors not because of what you expect to receive in return, but rather because it is what you feel you need or want to do.

Exercise 2-3: Attachment or Detachment?

List the past five times you have done a favor or given a gift. Look at your motivation for doing so. Was your action dictated by obligation? Did you have an expectation of what you would receive in return or an idea of what your desired outcome would be?

If your answer was "Yes" to either of these questions, you did not act with detachment. Giving freely and openly is not done with any expectation of receiving something in return.

Attachment to the outcome is often due to emotional baggage we carry, such as issues of responsibility and obligation or feelings of guilt. Addressing these issues can resolve the attachments and make it easier to live in the present moment. Detachment happens in the present moment.

Another example of not living with detachment is over-involvement with the lives of others. To live others' problems, to match their emotions, and to invest in the outcome of their lives is an exercise in futility. (In the end they make their own choices anyway.) This behavior pulls us completely out of *our* present moment. It is appropriate to be compassionate, empathetic, and loving to others in their times of need. However, when we are no longer with them, our focus should return to the moments of *our* lives. It is in this way that we truly remain able to stay compassionate, empathetic, and loving.

Claiming Our Power

As emotional, energetic beings, we need to be aware of where we have invested our energy and to realize the necessity of releasing ourselves from those ties that disempower us. The energy of our thoughts and emotions affects our physical bodies. In Caroline Myss' book, *Anatomy of the Spirit*, she states, "Keep in mind that at all times your *biography* becomes your *biology*."

Our biography is our life story. Along with the positive experiences in our lives, our biography may consist of past or present traumatic experiences, relationships, and negative beliefs.

These things are our "baggage." Our biology is, of course, our bodies. What is meant by "your biography becomes your biology" is that your body is affected by your life story and your baggage. (We will discuss more fully the creation of baggage and how it affects the physical body in Section Three.)

**In order to truly claim your authentic power,
you must heal yourself of your baggage.**

Picture yourself as an octopus. You have eight arms. You are using one arm to hold onto the experience of a past trauma, say an auto accident. Three arms hold onto the pain of your mother's death, two arms hold onto the memory of a relationship gone bad, one arm holds onto problems at work, and so on. Do you see the point? It takes energy to keep your baggage alive. If, as an octopus, you are using all your arms to hold onto the past, how will you move or eat?

Now look at yourself. How much of your vital energy is available to you in the present? How much energy are you using to keep alive old wounds from your past? How much energy does your body have left to use to stay healthy, happy, and fulfilled? How much energy do you have to commit to present-day relationships with your spouse, children, parents, siblings, friends, and coworkers?

**Reclaiming your power occurs when you look at where you
give your power away and begin to resolve those issues.**

As an emotional, energetic being, be aware of where you have invested your energy and realize the necessity of releasing those ties (baggage) that disempower you! It is hard to walk lightly and smoothly through your life when you are lugging a suitcase full of emotional baggage.

Forgiveness

Forgiveness may be the most powerful technique in achieving a state of detachment. Forgiveness is a very effective process for reclaiming power. Many people operate under the misperception that forgiving is about the other person. Actually, it is about ourselves. The process of forgiveness is about making peace with the past. Marianne Williamson in her book *Return to Love* states, "Forgiveness is the key to inner peace because it is the mental technique by which our thoughts are transformed from fear to love."

Forgiveness is the choice to live in the present by releasing our judgments of past events and the negative emotions associated with them.

Holding onto anger, judgment, fear, and resentment toward people and situations in our past only keeps us attached to them. This prevents us from living the happy, fulfilled present moments of our lives. This is how holding onto negative emotions and judgments affects us. The negativity is actual energy and *it is in us* and lowers our vibrational frequency and drags us down. Forgiveness is one tool we can use that allows us to let go and move on.

Forgiveness is one of the highest frequency emotions and arises from a state of love and humility. It does not come from a place of superiority or the mentality of "What a wonderful person I am to forgive you." It comes from recognizing that, in forgiving another, we forgive ourselves. At the very least, we forgive ourselves for giving another this power over us and allowing ourselves to feel like victims.

In order to call our energy back from its attachment to another, we need to forgive, let go, and detach.

Exercise 2-4: Feeling forgiveness

At day's end prior to going to sleep, sit on the edge of your bed and take the opportunity to review your day. Look at any situations or interactions that have occurred about which you are still feeling emotional. Now look specifically at emotions you know can affect your energy negatively. Is there anything about which you feel judgment, anger, hurt, guilt, jealousy, shame, or resentment? Any other emotions? Now is a good time to address these issues. Looking at the concept that these experiences are really opportunities to learn about yourself, others, and life in general, take this time to check in. Did these experiences and interactions *mirror* any qualities about you and how you are living your life? Did you overreact about anything today? If your answer is "Yes" to these questions, acknowledge to yourself what lessons you can learn. Let go, in a loving fashion, of all that you can. Take it even one step further and acknowledge those particular lessons for which you can be grateful. Remember that these experiences are now in your past (even though it is your *recent* past). Thinking about them, especially repeatedly, infuses them with your energy and robs that energy from your present. *Call back this energy! Reclaim it for yourself! This is forgiveness!*

Forgiveness means letting go of any negativity you are harboring against others and letting go of the emotions you are sending their way. Forgive yourself, too, for holding onto these thoughts and emotions in the first place. Once again, be grateful for this opportunity and for the understanding you now have. Congratulations! You have just reclaimed your power!

We learn many of life's lessons through our interactions with others. This simple process of forgiveness can effectively release the emotional ties to events that have occurred. The purpose behind this process is to *call our spirits back* and to *empower ourselves* by eliminating those energetic ties that drain our vital energy.

Relationships

At one time or another most of us desire to have someone special, a chosen partner in life. Have you ever wondered how you actually choose that special person? You have in mind a list of the qualities, characteristics, traits, and physical attributes that you are looking for in another. It is with this list that you go hunting for a mate. Anytime you meet people, even though you may be unaware of the process, you automatically compare them to your checklist. You will usually acknowledge the potential for a person to be your special someone if he or she meets the majority of the criteria on your list. You tell yourself, "I like this person. She has most of the qualities I have been looking for." *What you don't realize is that you have chosen to overlook the qualities you find less than desirable.* These can come back to haunt you in the future.

Remember the phrase, "Mirror, mirror on the wall, who's the fairest one of all?" A new relationship with all its euphoria and feelings of love welling up inside we call the "Magic Mirror" phase. In this phase your entire outlook on life changes; everything seems wonderful. This happens because you are now acting very consciously. You are functioning from your conscious mind and are paying particular attention to what you say, what you do, and how you dress. You make these choices primarily because you want to present to this new special person the "Perfect You." *In reality this Magic Mirror is merely the illusion of perfection.*

Did you ever notice that after a while that perfect person doesn't seem so perfect anymore? What happens to cause that Magic Mirror to lose its luster? In the previous section we learned about perceptions and examined the reference list we carry in our minds. This is the list of information that has relevance to us. All individuals also have a perception of who they think they are, a list of all their good and bad traits. While in the Magic Mirror phase, we are consciously choosing to express only those traits we judge as "good" or "desirable." At the same time, the other person is doing the exact same thing!

As the relationship becomes more comfortable, we let down our guards. We stop being conscious of all our behaviors and begin to express from our subconscious. This is the "real us" and includes both the good stuff and the not-so-good stuff. Again, our partner is doing the same thing. As this person becomes more comfortable, he or she also starts expressing parts of himself or herself that up to this point have been kept hidden. We may ask ourselves, "What happened to that considerate, polite, thoughtful person who created the magic?" We call this the "Cracked Mirror" phase. It is a transition for you and your partner from the illusion of the "Perfect Person" to the reality of the "Whole Person." During this time, communication is doubly important. It is in this phase that you lay the groundwork for intimacy and true sharing, which are basic principles in a healthy relationship.

Mirroring

> **"All relationships are essentially a reflection of your relationship with yourself."—*Deepak Chopra***

The one-on-one relationship we have with our spouses or partners can actually be our greatest mirror. A lot of the traits our mates have we also possess. On the opposite side, often our mates provide the strength in our weak areas. They fill our gaps. If you are an insecure person, you will generally be attracted to someone who is secure or dominating. If you have a difficult time making up your mind, chances are you will choose a decisive mate. For these reasons, relationships can be our greatest teachers. Those who are close to us such as our mates, spouses, children, parents, and friends have a lot to teach us about ourselves. It is our emotional investment in those relationships that gives us an opportunity to interact with people who really matter to us. Those relationships can reflect our strengths and also our weaknesses. By becoming aware of our weaknesses, we can see the areas that need personal healing and growth. We can then work on, improve, and change them.

It is important to note that the process of looking at our weaknesses, or areas that we desire to change, is not a time to be judgmental. How many perfect people do we really know? Don't expect perfection in yourself either. Be as compassionate and gentle with yourself as you would be with another, even more so. Everyone, at some level, is in the process of self-discovery.

As you begin to realize that what you see in the people in your life is a reflection of yourself, you may start to see how you can use this information to then look at all areas of your life. Entertain the notion that you are responsible for creating your life and that the people and events are there to teach you about yourself.

You are the author of your existence.

This is a tremendous opportunity to use the concept of responsibility to bring about progressive and positive changes in your life. As you look deeply into your life and its experiences, remember that everything in it has or at one time had purpose. "Is it time to let it go?" "Has it served its purpose?" These become the questions to ask yourself. Make this process a loving process. Don't get caught up in guilt or condemnation when you answer these questions. Be willing to acknowledge and release those things that have served their purpose.

Exercise 2-5: Explore mirroring to learn about your life

Find a quiet, safe place to sit comfortably. Go inward and allow yourself to see how you feel about your life right now. Then look at the relationships in your life. What do they reflect? Are the people in your life loving, respectful, and honest, or are they angry, judgmental, and dishonest? Look at your home. Does it feel peaceful, nurturing, and beautiful, or does it feel chaotic, ugly, and upsetting? Look at your body. Does it reflect health, peace, and vitality or disease, fatigue, and stress? Look at your job, community, etc. Take this time to reflect fully on your life.

In areas where you feel negativity or you realize you desire change, look at what simple steps you can use to implement the changes you desire. Then look at long-term steps.

Remember to view this exercise as an opportunity. It is a time to be gentle, loving, and supportive of yourself.

Be aware that you are at least partially responsible for almost everything that exists in your life experience. Nothing is, or was, present by accident if it has served a purpose. Ask yourself whether this circumstance, person, or situation has served its purpose. Do you see clearly the reasons for it being in your life? Do you acknowledge and understand the lessons that have been available to you by having attracted it into your life in the first place? If your experience has resulted in frustration, it may be time to let it go. Be thoughtful and release yourself from it. Realize that you are doing your own inner work. Stay away from projecting your truth on others and trying to change them. Avoid the tendency to point your finger at others and be responsible for yourself.

**When you point your finger at someone else,
you have three fingers pointing back at yourself.**

Graciously accept yourself for being who and what you are in this moment and accept others for who they are, too. Detach from the need to be right and to make others wrong. Detach from the desire to "fix" your mate, family member, or friend.

Change begins with you. Be responsible for yourself and allow others the same courtesy. As you begin to take responsibility for yourself and your life, you will allow others to do the same. Demonstrate what you want to show up in your life and relationships. In other words, if you want to experience better communication with your child, become more communicative. If you want your spouse to be more affectionate, be more affectionate yourself. If you want your spouse to trust you, be trusting and trustworthy. Globally speaking, if you want more love and peace on earth, be more loving and peaceful.

Change begins with you.

Exercise 2-6: How do you feel about yourself?

In order to get a clear picture of how you see yourself, stand naked in front of a full-length mirror. Look at yourself from head to toe. Observe your feelings and reactions. How do you feel? Do you like and accept what you see? Are you loving or judgmental? Use this exercise as an opportunity to recognize things about yourself that no longer reflect who and what you are. If you have become more loving and accepting of yourself on the inside, does it carry over to your acceptance of yourself on the outside? If you have worked through issues of negativity such as anger, do you see that expressed in any way in your body? Does it look more relaxed? Is your face smoother? Are your shoulders less hunched? Step closer to the mirror, look yourself in the eye, and say, "I love you." How does that make you feel? If it makes you uncomfortable, you may want to reflect on how much you love and appreciate yourself.

If after doing this exercise you realize there are things about yourself that you judge or dislike, you have two choices: either accept these things and embrace them or decide to do what is necessary to lovingly change them so they are more acceptable to you.

Exercise 2-7: How do you feel about your mate?

To examine your relationship with your mate, stand toe to toe and look deeply into each other's eyes. Observe what you think and how you feel. Remember to observe, not judge. Again, this is an opportunity to choose growth and change by observing your thoughts and feelings, not an opportunity to judge or criticize yourself or your mate.

Communication

Understanding that we create emotion through our thoughts

and perceptions can release us from the tendency to point outward and blame others for what we are feeling. What we are
expressing and how we communicate it to others will affect their
response to us. When you are ready to communicate, be present, own your emotions, and express yourself from the first person perspective. Say, "I feel this when you say that," or "I felt
hurt and angry when you did that," as opposed to "You hurt my
feelings" or "You made me so angry." This may seem selfish, as
if you are making everything about you, but accurately verbal-
izing or expressing yourself actually facilitates communication
and helps prevent others from feeling offended or defensive.
Careful communication allows others to let down their walls
and to more comfortably express themselves. When you open
yourself up to other people, you are giving them the opportunity to open themselves up to you. As they sense your willing-
ness to be vulnerable, they may become more willing to be vulnerable, too. It is through communication that you will find
true intimacy with others.

Communication involves expressing yourself *and listening to
others*. When listening, strive to hear and feel what the other
person is trying to share. Listen without attachment and stay
present. *Don't miss the sharing because you are busy mentally com-
posing your next point.*

Communication Type

What follows is an evaluation of different types of commu-
nication/learning styles. It is very helpful for everyone in your
household to do this evaluation. We all have different styles of
communication. To be able to really communicate effectively,
we need to understand each other's type as well as our own.

Find Your Basic Communication Type*:

Number each of the following statements from "1" to "4." Use number "1" for those statements that least describe you and number "4" for those statements that best describe you. Write the number in the blank provided.

1. I make important decisions based on:
   (k) _____ gut-level feelings.
   (a) _____ which way sounds the best.
   (v) _____ what looks the best to me.
   (d) _____ precise diligent study of the issues.

2. During an argument, I am most likely to be influenced by:
   (a) _____ the other person's tone of voice.
   (v) _____ whether or not I can see the other person's point of view.
   (d) _____ the logic of the person's argument.
   (k) _____ whether or not I feel I am in touch with the other person's true feelings.

3. I most easily communicate what is going on with me by:
   (v) _____ the way I dress.
   (k) _____ the feelings I share.
   (d) _____ the words I choose.
   (a) _____ my tone of voice.

4 It is easy for me to:
   (a) _____ find the ideal volume and tuning on a stereo system.
   (d) _____ select the most intellectually relevant points concerning an interesting subject.

* Compliments of Infinity Institute International, Inc.-School of Hypnosis, www.infinityinst.com

(k) ___ select superbly comfortable furniture.

(v) ___ select rich color combinations.

5. I:

(a) ___ am very attuned to the sounds in my surroundings.

(d) ___ am very adept at making sense of new facts and data.

(k) ___ am very sensitive to the way articles of clothing feel on my body.

(v) ___ have a strong response to colors and the way a room looks.

Scoring:

To find your communication type, add together all the numbers that have the letter (a) next to them. Do the same for the letters (v), (k), and (d). You now have four totals, one for each of the four types: a=auditory, v=visual, k=kinesthetic, and d=digital.

Your highest total number of points indicates your communication type. It is also common to be higher in two areas. Your communication type is also your learning style. It is important to understand these styles for yourself and those around you.

Visual:

If you are strong in the visual channel, you are a person who:
- Likes to keep written records
- Typically reads billboards while driving or riding
- Follows written instructions, directions, or recipes
- Reviews for a test by writing a summary
- Is a bookworm
- Is a list maker

You also tend to express yourself verbally, using words and expressions such as:

An eyeful	Focus	Plainly see
Sight for sore eyes	Appears	Hindsight
Bird's eye view	Recognize	Eye to eye
Outlook	Tunnel vision	See to it

Kinesthetic:

If you are strong in the kinesthetic channel, you are a person who:
- Likes to build things
- Uses free time for physical activities
- Doodles and draws
- Enjoys the outdoors
- Loves crafts and handwork
- Feels textures

You also tend to express yourself verbally, using words and expressions such as:

All washed up	Texture	Comfortable
Feel/Felt	Touched	Rubbed me wrong
Hand-in-hand	Cold/hot	Sensitive

Auditory:

If you are strong in the auditory channel, you are a person who:
- Prefers listening to someone else read instructions or directions to you
- Studies by reading out loud or talking with others
- Prefers books on tape to reading
- Is able to concentrate deeply on what another is saying

- Uses rhyming words to remember names
- Loves talking with others

You also tend to express yourself verbally, using words and expressions such as:

Express yourself	Unheard of	Listen
Clear as a bell	Loud and clear	Discuss
Overhear	Power of speech	Exclaim/shout

Digital:

If you are strong in the digital channel, you are a person who:
- Works problems out in your mind first
- Mentally organizes lists
- Is very logical
- Does well in mathematics and science
- Conceptualizes abstracts
- Often observes rather than participates

You also tend to express yourself verbally, using words and expressions such as:

Think	Process	Organize
Know	Figure out	Problematic
Understand	Confusion	Thoughtful

Communication Type Summary

If you would like to explore or strengthen other types and styles of communication, try using words that are common for that style. Also, you can now see why it is important to understand the other styles you encounter in those people close to you. If you feel that ineffective communication is a problem between you and others, look at your communication styles. If they are different, it would be helpful to express yourself in a way they can understand. In other words, if you are visual, a list to *look* at may be the best way for you to understand. However, if the other person is auditory, he or she may need to *hear* the list read in order to fully comprehend. Ineffective communication due to different styles is often a stumbling block in relationships. By understanding the differences, you have one more tool to help you communicate easily and effectively.

Section Two Highlights:

- Emotions are energy frequencies, and each vibrates at a different rate.
- Emotions, thoughts, and body sensations combine to create our "feelings."
- Anger, fear, and hatred vibrate slower and make us feel heavier, dull, and dense.
- Emotions such as love, compassion, and joy vibrate faster and make us feel lighter.
- Honoring our emotions means acknowledging them without judgment so they may flow through us rather than creating an energetic block.
- A multisensory person is one who has full use of his or her five senses and the ability to "sense" energy. This person trusts intuition, hunches, and feelings.
- When we sense energy, we can use it as a barometer. Something either feels good (comfort), or it does not (discomfort).
- Stress is often the result of attachment. When we are attached to something or to an outcome and our expectation goes unmet, the result can be stress.
- The only constant in life is change.
- Detachment is letting go of those things that are not relevant in the present moment.
- It takes vital energy to keep our baggage alive.
- The act of forgiveness is done for ourselves rather than another.

- Our relationships to the people and things in our lives mirror aspects of ourselves. (These may be traits we have or may not have but desire to have.)
- Careful communication allows all parties to share their thoughts and feelings without blame or judgment.
- There are four basic communication types that are also learning styles. They are visual, kinesthetic, auditory, and digital.

Section Three:

The Physical

"You are only dreaming that you have a body of flesh. Your real self is light and consciousness … The body is simply a projection of that invisible self within."

—Paramahansa Yogananda

"For every state of consciousness, there is a corresponding state of physiology."

—Deepak Chopra

Putting It Together

In Section One we introduced the concept that we are all thinking, conscious beings who assimilate information filtered and based upon our perceptions. In Section Two we discovered that the resulting beliefs and attitudes create our emotions and that each emotion has its own vibrational frequency. In Section Three we will present the concepts of the physical. We will show you how your physical body and your level of health are impacted by your mental and emotional processes.

Consider the example of a roller coaster ride. Did you know that the response of your physical body to a roller coaster ride is based on your attitude? The person who approaches it with tremendous enthusiasm and thinks it will be great fun has a different physical response than the person who approaches the experience with doubt and fear. As the roller coaster crests that first big hill, the first person by her level of excitement and enjoyment creates within her brain a release of chemicals such as serotonin and endorphins. These will in turn bring about an even higher sense of elation and joy. This actually has an uplifting effect on her physical body and causes it to function more efficiently.

The second person is afraid. He has concerns for his personal safety. As the roller coaster drops over the first hill, this person experiences increased levels of apprehension. His body in turn is flooded with neurochemicals such as adrenaline and norepindephrine. These chemicals create an additional physical stress on his body.

The same activity can create two entirely different personal physical experiences. Each experience is based upon how the individual's thoughts, perceptions, and emotions manifest themselves into body chemistry that can actually be felt physically. Our bodies experience what we think and feel. A mind under stress is a body under stress. Likewise, the reverse is also true. An enthusiastic state of mind creates positive, elevated effects on the body.

Our minds and bodies are so intimately connected that what our minds think our bodies feel.

The "fight or flight" response experienced when encountering something perceived as a potential danger clearly illustrates the dramatic and rapid changes that are experienced in our bodies as we prepare to "flee" or "do battle." These typically include increased heart rate and blood pressure, an increase in strength and muscle tone, expansion of bronchial tubes for more effective respiration, dilation of the pupils, and even enhanced sensory skin sensations to better assess and react to the situation. This is the fuel that the body needs to perform at peak capacity during times of danger or crisis. This heightened awareness, along with increased body functioning, is what it took to carry out the rescues on September 11, 2001. Whether caring for others or just trying to take care of themselves, it took a fully functioning "fight or flight" response for all people involved to reach safety.

conscious → subconscious → unconscious

We each assess any and every situation to which we are exposed with our capabilities of logic, rationale, and judgment. These capabilities, however, are filtered by our perceptions. One person's perception of a big dog running toward him or her may be entirely different than the perception of someone else. It depends on each person's past experience with a "big dog." This experience may be perceived as a pleasant or a fearful one;

therefore, the body reactions will also be entirely different, just as on the roller coaster ride.

Did you know that tears of sadness and tears of joy have different chemical compositions? The body response of tears can be triggered by entirely different emotions. The tears will actually carry the chemistry of the emotion that triggered the response! The mind and body are so intimately connected that what our minds think our bodies feel.

Real vs. Pretend

Our subconscious minds do not know the difference between real and pretend. This is why when we are reading a book or watching a movie, we are able to so vividly experience the emotions that are being expressed. As we feel the sadness, joy, or horror, so do our bodies. When we give ourselves permission to set aside our conscious minds and imagine or "buy into" the story, we are opening our subconscious to the experience *as if it were real.* This is why our bodies react with tears, laughter, or tension even though intellectually we know it is "just a story."

Exercise 3-1: Remembering a lemon

When doing this exercise, be comfortable. If you need to be alone to fully apply yourself, then be alone. Read through this exercise first; then, do it.

Close your eyes and picture yourself standing in front of your house while you are looking at your front door. Engage all your senses. Do you feel wind or a warm sun? How does the ground feel? What does your house look like? Walk slowly to the door, grasp the knob, turn it, open the door, and enter your house. Walk into your kitchen; again engage all your senses. Go to the refrigerator and get out a lemon. Feel the lemon; it is cold. What is the texture, the shape? Is it round or oblong, with those knobs on the ends? Gently squeeze it. Is it firm or soft? Take it to the counter and set it on a cutting board; pick up a knife and cut it in half. Smell it as you cut. Does the juice squirt out? Now pick up the lemon; put it to your nose and inhale deeply. Open your mouth and take a bite.

Notice your body's response. You have a memory of the experience of a lemon. Your body just responded to this experience even though it was not really happening.

How the subconscious works and its awesome power are important concepts to grasp. An understanding of the subconscious allows us to see how athletes who use visualization are often more accomplished and why doctors such as Bernie Siegel have had success when teaching patients to use visualization to heal even such serious diseases as cancer. Through the lemon exercise, you just experienced how your subconscious mind really doesn't know the difference between real and pretend. This is precisely why you need to choose carefully what you are willing to program into your subconscious. Look at your choices in entertainment. You are exposed to messages and programming through television and movies, books and magazines, and even song lyrics. We have already examined the concept of advertising and how it can contribute to the creation of perceptions and filters. It is the same with entertainment and even the news media. Where do you draw the line? It is different for each person. What is important to understand is how different types of input affect you, personally, and that you need to make your choices accordingly.

Back in Section One we learned that children do not even develop their conscious minds until after age seven. Up until this point they operate out of their subconscious minds, which, as you know, do not have the ability to differentiate between real and pretend. This is why children can lose themselves so completely when engrossed in television. *To them it is real!* Children are unable to separate fact from fiction. That is why they fear monsters under the bed and believe in the tooth fairy. They do not have fully developed conscious minds. It is the adults in children's lives who must take the responsible role of helping them to assimilate the world around them. This means making choices regarding the appropriateness or inappropriateness of the "messages" they receive on a daily basis. When our children are young, we are their first line of defense and their primary filter.

The Creation of "Baggage"

What our minds think our bodies feel. Emotional pain causes physical pain. A mind under stress is a body under stress. Understanding that as children we are unable to separate fact from fiction or real from pretend is the beginning of understanding just how baggage is created. As children we do not understand sarcasm. We do not understand when things are "understated" or "overstated." We do not understand that things said in anger or pain are not necessarily the true feelings of the person speaking. As young children, we do not have the ability to discern for ourselves whether or not we will choose to believe something. What we hear we believe to be true. The circumstances in our lives are also out of our control. It is not in our control whether our parents have more children, lose jobs, move, or divorce. We just feel the effects and live with the results.

**As children, we have a way of internalizing
everything in our world and making it about us.**

Was your childhood perfect? If it wasn't, you undoubtedly

felt that it was a reflection of you and your imperfections. This is a good example of why so often young children feel responsible if their parents divorce. The children internalize the situation along with any fights or conversations they may have overheard. If they have misbehaved recently, they may look at that as a reason and feel at fault. By the time the divorce occurs, there are generally many instances for children to have gathered and misinterpreted information. No wonder we have baggage!

Most of the possibilities for us to assume baggage as a child grow out of our innocence. As we grow older, we are more responsible. That in and of itself can cause baggage. We make choices. They may be poor ones. We may hurt people. We may be hurt. We may experience loss. We may betray someone. We may be betrayed. Each person will respond to these circumstances differently. Some may carry extreme sadness and low self-esteem and slide through life not wanting to be noticed. Others may be fueled by the injustices they perceive and become angry and aggressive and demand attention. The reactions are as diverse as there are numbers of people. Most people have in place some type of defense mechanism, or way to protect themselves, that will allow them to go on and deal with their lives and the circumstances that have shaped them.

We all carry or have carried baggage. We all deserve to heal. Healing occurs when we make the choice to address our issues and emotional baggage. (Often it is necessary to have a trained therapist help us.) Many people put off making this choice until their baggage and the stress of carrying it has created actual physical disease, or dysfunction, in their bodies. By healing our wounds, we allow ourselves the opportunity to gain an understanding of who we are and how we can become the person we desire to be. This is the path to wholeness and happiness, and it is our choice to make.

Exercise 3-2: Feeling comfort/discomfort

Make a list of things that strongly affect you and bring on feelings of negativity. Are you angry at your mother or spouse? Do you have a history of abuse? Have you experienced a recent death or loss? As you identify these issues and circumstances, observe how your body feels. Do you feel comfort or discomfort? Are these healthy, positive changes in your body? Do you want to keep these feelings any longer?

If your answer is "No," you need to do some healing work. We urge you to find a qualified alternative or traditional healing practitioner in your area to help you.

Growth vs. Protection

It was in the early 1990s at Stanford University that researchers in the area of cell control mechanisms made an amazing discovery. They discovered that the behavior of a cell is determined by the receptors on the surface of the cell and that the information gathered by these receptors comes from the cell's environment. In other words, a liver cell is a liver cell because it is in the liver and surrounded by liver cells and liver cell information.

This is a very important piece of information. We have learned that we see the world through the filter of our thoughts, perceptions, and attitudes and that they make up the environment of our minds. With this new information, we are better able to see that what is the environment of our minds is then also the environment of our bodies.

An organism's perception conforms to its environment.

Researchers further determined that a cell is able to be in a mode of growth or a mode of protection but not both at the same time. Because our bodies are made up of our cells, we need to look at this information as it relates to the whole organism, our whole bodies. We then see that this principle at work in our bodies and our lives indicates that we are able to be in a mode of growth and evolution or a mode of protection, fear, and stagnation.

Growth is easy to understand. It is the progression and development of our systems, beliefs, and processes. Growth implies a constant state of change. In a state of growth people are evolving, hopefully improving, but nonetheless moving forward in their lives.

Protection is a response to fear. It is a perception, or feeling, that we need to protect ourselves. The more we move into this place of fear, the less we can grow. It's not even surprising that this is such a common and, unfortunately, comfortable space. Look at the environment in which we live. Western society as a whole looks to the military as "protection" from foreign invaders; we look to the police to "protect" us from criminals; we lock and bolt our doors; we put in car alarms; we even teach our children to fear strangers. These are all beliefs and actions due to our notions of protection and fear. To a large degree, the structure of Western society is based on circumstances of protection and fear. Even the widely embraced theory of evolution that has been taught in our schools says that only the strong survive. So we strive to be bigger, better, and stronger, but the reason we do this is often based on fear although we seldom recognize this.

There are many forms of fear. Most of the emotions we call "negative" stem from fear. Shame, blame, judgment, greed, rage, and hatred are examples of fear-based emotions. They have a lower vibrational frequency, which affects our physical bodies.

There are also the issues of abandonment, rejection, and death that can strike fear into our hearts. These emotions and issues are often painful, unhealed wounds that have become emotional baggage. If you are carrying around emotional baggage, it is based on issues of fear and puts you in a state of protection. Growth and protection are at opposite ends of the spectrum. It is easy to see why we can be in either a mode of growth and evolution or a mode of protection, fear, and stagnation. If you recognize yourself as being in a state of protection, notice whether or not you are open to change. There are many types of therapy that are available to help individuals sort through and resolve the mental and emotional issues that keep them stuck in protection. By addressing your baggage, you open yourself to the growth mode and begin a journey of true healing.

A mind under stress is a body under stress, and a body under stress is a body out of balance.

Negative emotions and living in protection can lower the vibrational frequency of our bodies for extended periods of time. This lower frequency energy affects even our routine physical body functions. Remember, as long as we are living in a mode of protection, so are our cells. Therefore, living in protection directly affects how the body regenerates and heals itself and how it expresses health and wholeness. Even healthy bodies are the home for germs, bacteria, and viruses. However, in a stress-free body they do not flourish. If our bodies become stressed and out of balance, these organisms are given the opportunity to multiply and can result in disease.

Is our health a choice? Is the health of our bodies up to us? To a large degree, yes! There are many ways to care for ourselves, reduce stress, and move toward greater health and wholeness.

These include:
- Awareness of thoughts and self-talk
- Using affirmations to improve our attitudes
- Healing our emotional wounds
- Letting go and forgiving
- Good nutrition and exercise
- Proper rest and relaxation
- Allowing time each day for quiet time, prayer, and meditation

Mind/Body Connections

The International Medical and Dental Hypnotherapy Association™ has as its goal the vision of a hypnotherapist on staff at every hospital. The good news is that this is beginning to happen. This organization, along with many others, recognizes the huge potential for healing when bringing the body and mind together in the treatment process and is working hard to bring this vision forward for the benefit of us all.

In her book *Heal Your Body*, author Louise Hay gives the probable mental cause for many different physical illnesses. Her book suggests positive mental thoughts that can be substituted for negative ones. This concept brings together much of what we have learned so far. Basically, she is using the conscious mind, through affirmations, to access the subconscious and gain entry into the unconscious for physical healing.

conscious → subconscious → unconscious

Cell biologist Bruce Lipton, Ph.D., has studied the chemical receptors that physically exist in the outer walls and membranes of cells. These receptors interact with the neurochemicals and hormones circulating through the body *that are produced as a result of thoughts and emotions.* This makes sense when we look at the roller coaster example. The thoughts and emotions each person experienced created certain physical changes in his or her body. These changes resulted in the release of certain hormones and chemicals. Through Dr. Lipton's research, we can see that these hormones and neurochemnicals interact directly with chemical receptors on the surface of cells. This is proof that our thoughts and emotions affect our cells, and since our body is made up of cells, these are actual detailed mind-body connections at work.

Another researcher in this area is Candace Pert, Ph.D. She is a research professor in the department of physiology and biophysics at Georgetown University Medical Center in Washington, D.C., and has extensively studied the dynamic system that links mind and body. The author of *Molecules of Emotion,* Dr. Pert is responsible for isolating and trapping the small morphine molecule on its receptor. The discovery of this previously unknown opiate receptor has had far-reaching effects extending into almost every field of medicine. In addition, it has helped to bring together the fields of psychology and biology.

It is through the work of dedicated scientists such as Dr. Lipton and Dr. Pert that there is now proof of the connection between our thoughts, feelings, emotions, and our physical health.

Treatment of the Body

There is currently a shift happening in Western medicine. Historically, Western medicine has focused on body function while, separately, psychotherapy has focused on the mind (and religion has focused on spiritual). Until recently, the strength of Western medicine has been largely in diagnosis rather than treatment. When focused on treatment, it has generally addressed symptoms concerned with how disease expresses itself in the body. There are specialists for practically every body part and function, and doctors often treat each part separately. In the past, traditional medical treatment has generally been invasive, rather than looking at lifestyle changes. The recognition is emerging, however, that health and wholeness are the result of a balance between the mental, emotional, physical, and spiritual aspects. Finding this balance and addressing it along with the individual health of each area brings greater wholeness. This new approach suggests that the root cause of disease or illness may often be something other than physical. While it may generally still be necessary to treat the physical body, attention paid to the mental, emotional, and spiritual aspects as well may allow for a more complete healing.

It is now common to see birth centers where families participate together in the entire emotional and physical experience of the gift of life. It has become more common for oncology and cardiac care units to offer biofeedback, meditation, and yoga classes as avenues to begin treatment of the mental and emotional counterparts of many chronic physical diseases. Guided imagery and visualization are being used in pain management with remarkable results. There are also an increasing number of studies substantiating the positive healing effects resulting from group consciousness, such as blessings and prayer. These alternatives are not yet commonplace and there are many others that are not even recognized, but Western society is slowly moving forward.

In this culture many of us have learned to treat our symptoms rather than look for the cause or encourage our bodies to utilize their own innate wisdom. There may be a tendency to feel we don't have the time to let our bodies do their own healing. Maybe we are too busy. For instance, one of the ways the body gets rid of toxins is by making mucus. This then creates an avenue for the toxin to leave the body. A common reaction is to think we can't be bothered by the symptoms of excess mucus such as a sore throat or runny nose. Instead, we may ingest something to dry up the mucus. This makes us feel better by suppressing the body's attempts to cleanse itself, but where does the toxin go? How does it get out of the body? And what about the stuff we just put into our bodies? What does the body do with that? Fortunately, our bodies know what they need to do and will often let the toxin lie dormant for a while before they try, once again, to release it. But if our attitudes haven't changed, the pattern won't either. If we still feel we don't have time, we will just keep treating the symptoms and suppressing the body's attempts to heal itself. If this cycle is familiar to you, it may be time to stop and look at your health and how you *treat* your body.

Do you believe that health is really just the absence of symptoms? If you recognize this as a belief you hold, is it one you wish to keep? To be truly healthy, there must be a point at which you are willing to address the causes of disease and illness, rather than just be satisfied with suppressing the symptoms. You may have already reached that point, but if not, how about starting now?

Primitive cultures such as the Mayans and traditional Eastern philosophies of medicine such as Chinese or Indian treat the individual as a whole being. They recognize each person as unique, having his or her own body type, size, and weight and also having his or her own personal emotional, mental, and spiritual sides. These traditions of medicine focus on finding and working with the underlying causes of disease. In these older, more traditional types of treatments, you would never receive a prescription for some premade, universal, "one size fits all" pill. Instead, you would take individual herbs in the proper dose for you or perhaps several combined and made into tea. Typically, you would also look at your lifestyle to see what changes you could implement there. Our Western society has much to learn from this simpler, more traditional method of health care.

Nervous System Function

Ponder for a moment the function of the nervous system. The brain, spinal cord, and all the peripheral nerves act as a communication system and directly or indirectly control all the functions of the physical body. Our brains tell our body parts what to do, and the body parts report back to the brain their changes and functions. On one hand, the transmission of nerve signals appears to be a rapid series of chemical changes in the neurons and synapses, but what is actually being transmitted is intelligence and information in the form of electrical impulses. These life-sustaining nerve functions are an expression of non-physical consciousness and information, coupled with physical and biological actions.

Consider the simple movement of bending an arm. A nerve impulse in the brain travels down the spinal cord and exits the spine in the neck region. It moves out the shoulder and down the arm and travels to the appropriate muscle groups. When stimulated, the muscles contract and shorten and cause the arm bones, which are hinged at the elbow joint, to move toward each other. This causes the arm to bend. All this is done in a millisecond without our awareness. We have a thought, "I need to catch that falling glass" (conscious). The thought may be fueled by emotion, perhaps anger or fear in this case (subconscious). The body responds appropriately, and the arm moves, reaches, and catches (unconscious). From the thoughts in our conscious minds to the response of our bodies, we are usually unaware of this entire process.

conscious → subconscious → unconscious

The idea that there is a life-enhancing, innate intelligence that functions through our nervous system is the basic principle on which the chiropractic healing profession is based. Most chiropractors agree that this innate intelligence is the expression of the divine essence within and that it coordinates and integrates our body functions and brings about healing, homeostasis, and all the countless body and cellular functions.

The proper function of the spine and nervous system is the focus of the chiropractic profession. Doctors of chiropractic ensure proper function of the spinal column by finding and correcting spinal subluxations. A spinal subluxation is a misalignment of the spinal column that adversely affects the supply of vital nerve impulses that creates body malfunction, symptoms, and disease.

The nonphysical consciousness that operates through our nervous system is our life force. Proof of this is seen when the brain is deprived of oxygenated blood for eight minutes or more. As the brain ceases to function, the physical body dies, and the spirit, or life force, leaves the body. Could it be that who and what we are is really not physical at all?

Who we really are is the emotional, mental, and spiritual aspects of our being residing in a physical form.

The Physical Body

The physical body is in a constant state of cellular regeneration. In his book *Quantum Healing*, Deepak Chopra says: "If you could see your body as it really is, you would never see it the same way twice. Ninety-eight percent of the atoms in your body were not there a year ago. The skeleton that seems so solid was not there three months ago. The configuration of the bone cells remains somewhat constant, but atoms of all kinds pass freely back and forth through the cell walls, and thereby that means you acquire a new skeleton every three months. The skin is new every month. You have a new stomach lining every five minutes. The cells in the liver turn over very slowly, but new atoms still flow through them, like water in a river course, making a new liver every six weeks."

The very cells that make up our bodies are in a constant state of death and regeneration. This understanding raises some critical questions. Why do we keep the same aches, pains, illnesses, and diseases? If the body itself is changing and regenerating, how can ill health remain? Research has proven that the makeup of a cell is determined by its environment, and much of that environment is made up of mental and emotional states. Do we stay sick simply because our perception of ourselves is as a person with a certain illness or disease? What about our baggage? Are our bodies carrying around "unhealthy" energy in the form of thoughts and emotions?

Matter

In 1913 Niels Bohr, a Danish physicist, developed the familiar model of the atom. It is a model that is still taught today. In science class many of us learned that the smallest component of all physical things is the atom. We were taught that the atom has a nucleus made up of positive and neutrally charged particles and that this nucleus is surrounded by orbiting layers of negatively charged particles called electrons. These tiny, seemingly solid atoms make up all the parts of our physical bodies and all the "things" in our physical world. Atoms are often called the building blocks of all matter.

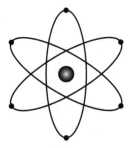

Technological advances such as the development of the electron microscope in 1931 allowed the atom to be viewed under greater magnification than ever before. In fact, there is now the ability with a transmission electron microscope to magnify a specimen fifty to one million times. This capability is what led to the discovery that the nucleus of the atom is actually composed of subatomic particles called positrons and even smaller particles called quarks. As researchers continued to investigate the possibilities of even smaller and smaller particles of matter, they made an astounding discovery that rocked the scientific world. Conclusive evidence has proven that, at its most minute level, these subatomic "particles" that make up all physical matter are really not solid at all! The electrons of an atom are not really negatively charged particles, but rather they are tiny bundles of electrical energy.

Electrons are actual *clouds* of negatively charged energy that orbit a positively charged nucleus, and *none of it is actually solid!*

In essence, 99.99 percent of what we think of as solid matter is mostly empty space and energy. Something only appears to be solid because the molecules that make up that "thing" vibrate at such a slow rate that we can observe it with our eyes.

Even more mind boggling than subatomic structure is the fact that subatomic particles seem to be affected by thought.

Quarks are bits of energy so small that they cannot actually be "seen." What is actually observed and recorded is the energy trail left by a moving quark, much like the jet stream that remains in the sky long after a jet has passed. In the process of counting these energy trails, it was discovered that the activities of the quarks being observed were altered by the process of observation. In other words, the thoughts and intentions of the observer influenced what was being observed! Could it be that thought affects everything, even our external physical world?

Have you lived under the illusion that you are a physical being, living in a physical world? These new discoveries prove that the concept of a physical world made of solid matter is incorrect. In fact, nothing is solid! Everything is made of energy vibrating at different rates! Thought and intention are capable of influencing the smallest particles of matter!

The appearance of something as solid is merely an illusion.

When you truly understand and believe that what you think affects everything in your life, you come to a point at which you can choose change. Information such as this can become the starting point for new attitudes, beliefs, and filters. How could it not? Perhaps it will become less important to put value on things of the physical world, such as money and the material possessions it can buy. Perhaps more emphasis will be put on who you are, how you think, and what you have to offer the world. It's a nice thought, isn't it?

Physical Properties of Matter

The subconscious mind holds as truth our beliefs and perceptions. Questioning the way things seem to be is often necessary before change and growth can occur. People perceived the world as flat until Christopher Columbus attempted to sail to the edge and discovered the "New World." How many perceptions do you have about your physical reality that you just accept as being real? How often are you misled by the information you perceive about the physical world through your five senses? Physical science teaches that matter exists in one of three states: something is either a solid, liquid, or gas. Once again, this is something most of us know, and yet we probably have never before seen its relevance in daily life. We know that molecules are made of atoms, and it is how the atoms are structured that determines how a substance will appear in its natural state. The state of a physical substance is primarily the result of its vibrational frequency, or the energy (movement) of the molecules that make up that substance. The simplest substances, or elements, are gases because the molecules vibrate fast enough to appear invisible. More complex substances such as lead have heavy, slower moving molecules. They are dense and appear solid. In between are liquids that have a faster vibratory rate than solids but are slower than gases. They are visible but not solid.

A simple example of the different physical properties can be illustrated by looking at water (H_2O), or two atoms of hydrogen and one of oxygen. Ice is water in solid form. If you take an ice cube and put it into a pan, set it on the stove, and apply energy in the form of heat, the ice will begin to melt. What is happening is that the slow-moving water molecules in the ice are beginning to vibrate faster and becoming liquid. As energy is further applied, the liquid water molecules vibrate faster and faster until they become steam, or water vapor. This water substance is now an invisible gas. All three—ice, liquid water, and vapor—are H_2O that exists in different states due to the vibrational frequency of the molecules.

Fishermen through the ages have melted lead to pour into

molds and make sinkers. Even something as solid and heavy as lead can be influenced by energy and changed to liquid!

Look again at the perception that we live in a physical world. A world made up of the atoms and molecules of everything that surrounds us. What we see easily are the solids and liquids, and this reinforces our perception of the world as physical. We believe something to be solid because that is how it looks. In reality, we now know that what appears to be solid only appears that way because the atoms and molecules vibrate at a slow enough speed that they can be seen with the human eye. We have also learned that atoms are mostly empty space, so the perception of something as being solid is actually an illusion.

Time and Aging

In our world we have agreed to the idea of linear time. We are not even aware that we have agreed to this concept, but we have. It is based on our belief that circumstances and events must follow in a progressive linear fashion. It is interesting that scientists have theorized that in other galaxies and dimensions linear time, as we know it, may not even exist.

These concepts and beliefs about time actually affect our mental, emotional, and physical being. Western society seems largely based on measuring accomplishment to determine value. This has created people who rush around trying to accomplish more and more yet never seem to have enough time. These attitudes about time and accomplishment, and the behaviors resulting from holding and acting on these attitudes, can have obvious effects on mental and emotional well-being. This is one way emotional tension and stress are created, which then strongly affects physical health.

Preoccupation with the passage of time impacts our lives on a daily basis. Think of all the "time monitoring" devices commonly used today. In a modern kitchen you can generally find clocks on the coffee maker, stove, and microwave. Watches come in any price and style. Chances are you have a clock in your car, on your cell phone, and next to your bed. There are a large number of people who simply cannot function without their calendars and appointment books. But many supposed "time saving" inventions actually take a tremendous amount of time to learn how to use and maintain. The computer is a time-saving invention. However, to become a proficient user *takes a long time*. Even purchasing a new washer and dryer comes with its complications. Now, when you do the laundry, first you have to choose from several different cycles, settings, and temperatures. When you purchase a new television, you must learn how to set the stations and the language, not just the tint and color. Even the telephone, which used to be a pretty basic instrument, has become something that needs to be learned and programmed.

Simplifying our lives by using modern inventions sure has become complicated and takes a lot of time!

Living in the present moment means appreciating the here and now, this moment, this sunset, this opportunity to connect with a loved one. It also means experiencing unpleasantness in this moment and then moving on. As you begin to live more in the present moment, you relinquish your attachment to past events and your worries and concerns of how you picture your future. We have encouraged you to be aware of your thoughts, words, and attitudes, and you have learned the importance of clearing your energy and healing your baggage. This process allows you to move toward the concept of living in the present moment. It's a great place to be!

Minutes lead to hours, months, and years; this creates the illusion of a past, present, and future. In reality, all we really have is a successive series of present moments.

This notion of linear time, that circumstances and events follow in a progressive linear fashion, is also the basis of our beliefs regarding aging. Western society perpetuates the notion that as time marches on, we get older, we get sick, and we die. Have you ever stopped to question your beliefs about the passage of time?

Exercise 3-3: Your beliefs on aging

Sit alone in a quiet space. Read through each of the questions before answering. Take the time to write down your perceptions and feelings regarding each question. Remember, it is healthy to question your beliefs.

On your birthday, how do you celebrate the passage of yet another year? What is your attitude about your age and the aging process? Do you embrace life or consider it survival?

If you believe that you are getting older, does that actually contribute to the process of aging? If yes, identify the issues associated with this belief.

When you look around, do you see others growing older? Do you see your age reflected through the growth of those younger than you? How do these experiences affect your perception of your own age and aging process?

Do you ever notice the deterioration of your physical form without blaming it on old age or getting older? Are there mental and emotional stresses created by your lifestyle that could be responsible for the physical changes?

What are they, and what do you want to do about them?

The length of a person's life is not nearly as important as the quality of the life he or she chooses to live. It is difficult to see any healthy, positive benefits regarding Western society's concepts of aging. In many cultures such as the Mayan, Native American, and most Eastern traditions, as a person ages, he or she is regarded with reverence. These cultures acknowledge that the older a person becomes, the more wisdom he or she has to share. Aging is honored.

Western culture, on the other hand, values appearance. There is a tendency to fight against the aging of the body that is very often taken to extremes. There are the options of various types of face lifts to appear more youthful, liposuction to remove fat, breast enlargements to enhance the figure, botox treatments to erase lines, and the list goes on and on. What if instead of worrying about your appearance, you were able to spend your valuable energy keeping your body fit and healthy? What if you occupied the mind with positive challenges and celebrated the passing of each day with gratitude? *This is the process of growing gracefully into each successive day of your life.*

Feeling Challenged

Remember, what your mind thinks your body feels. Your very thoughts affect your physical body. Just as ice becomes water and water becomes steam by increasing the amount of energy applied to it, the physical world is absolutely influenced by the nonphysical properties of thought, energy, and spirit.

If your perception has always been that your physical world is solid and that time and aging are unquestionable, then you may be feeling as though your basic beliefs are being challenged.

The next section will explain in greater detail just how completely the physical world is connected to, and influenced by, nonphysical properties.

Section Three Highlights:

- ➻ Our minds and bodies are so intimately connected that what our minds think our bodies feel.
- ➻ A mind under stress is a body under stress.
- ➻ The actual chemical mixture present in our bodies at any given moment is in response to our thoughts, perceptions, and emotions.
- ➻ Our subconscious mind does not know the difference between real and pretend.
- ➻ Treatment of the body must take mental, emotional, and spiritual factors into account for optimal health.
- ➻ The physical body is in a constant state of regeneration.
- ➻ The life force that controls and integrates our bodies functions through the nervous system.
- ➻ We are able to be in a mode of growth or protection but not both at the same time.
- ➻ Growth is a natural state.
- ➻ Protection is a response to fear.
- ➻ Even the tiny atom is not solid.
- ➻ Empty space and energy make up 99.99 percent of what we think of as solid matter.
- ➻ The speed at which atoms vibrate, their vibratory rate, determines whether they appear as a solid, liquid, or gas.
- ➻ Our preoccupation with time can keep us from living in the present moment.

Section Four:

The Spiritual

"There is something in every one of you that waits and listens for the sound of the genuine in yourself. It is the only true guide you will ever have. And if you cannot hear it, you will all of your life spend your days on the ends of strings that somebody else pulls."

—Howard Thurman

"We shape clay into a pot, but it is the emptiness inside that holds whatever we want."

—Tao Te Ching

What to Call It?

When talking about molecules vibrating at a certain rate, or vibratory frequency, it is easy to label the nonphysical as energy. Talking about the life force within us and the organizing structure of the universe, however, causes some people to experience deep-seated feelings and emotions. When referring to the organizing force of creation, we have chosen to use the term "God." If you do not feel comfortable with the word we have chosen, simply substitute another. Recognize, however, that if a simple word has such an emotional impact, there may be an issue around it that represents emotional baggage. For many, this is the patriarchal image of a God figure who sits in judgment. For others, it results from having religious rules imposed upon you as a child or time away from play for church attendance. There are as many reasons as there are people, but if your desire is to examine your personal issues and emotional baggage, this is another opportunity to observe what issues or negativity you may be carrying.

Exercise 4-1: Feelings about creation

What feelings does the word "God" bring up in you? Are they positive or negative? Is it the concept of God in general or just the word that makes you feel the way you do? Reflect a moment on your belief in a universal intelligence or organizing force of creation. What does it mean to you?

Our Nonphysical Reality: Technology

In the previous section the difference between the familiar Newtonian atom and the new model of a Quantum atom was discussed. We learned that the belief in a physical world made up of solid particles is false. In fact, nothing is solid at all! Everything that appears as solid is actually mostly empty space. By learning this, we can expand our view of the universe. We can now choose to eliminate limitations we may have experienced as a result of not having all the information. This new vision can also help us get in touch with the nonphysical element that may have been missing in our lives. It is very easy to stay separated from the life force if we believe that we are only physical beings who are living a physical experience in a physical world.

Physical reality, as we perceive it, is essentially nonphysical.

All the latest technologies from microwaves and digital satellites to telecommunications involving fiber optics are rooted in nonphysical reality. Could our ancestors have ever imagined that fiber-optic technology would encode millions of bits of information on *light* and send it all through a strip of plastic no bigger than a wire? Thirty years ago few people realized that laser beams could be used in delicate surgical procedures. We have gone from observing bacteria under a microscope to harnessing the nonphysical power of light itself. These modern conveniences, listed below, are generally taken for granted, yet they all operate on the principles of nonphysical energy.

- Electricity
- Telephone
- Radio waves
- Laser technology
- Fiber optics
- Photography
- Cell phones
- Nuclear power
- Television
- Digital satellites

When an apple fell on Isaac Newton's head, the end result was his theories of gravity and motion. From the deep desire to communicate over long distances, Alexander Graham Bell realized the possibility of transmitting voice over electric wires. The quest for greater understanding seems to bring us, time after time, to the realization that invisible, energetic aspects are at the core of all things.

Inherent in these discoveries and technologies is the understanding that in the unseen, or nonphysical, there is power, energy, and information. There is vibration, and there is life, or the essence of life. The same is true of a human being. A body is made up of vibrating molecules, intelligence, and energy.

The essence of life is nonphysical.

Our Nonphysical Reality: Spirit

What is the life force within us? This essence—this "who" we really are—is nonphysical. It is our spirit. "Spirit" is the part of us that receives information from our senses (multisensory). It is our thoughts and emotions. It is our connection to God and the life force of creation that flows in all living things. It is, therefore, our connection (on a nonphysical level) with all life. We are spiritual (nonphysical) beings having a physical experience, rather than the other way around.

"Spirit" is the nonphysical essence of our beings.

A good example of this spiritual connection is prayer. Prayer is a combination of thought, intention, emotion, and a belief in the power of a universal intelligence, or God. Through prayer we send out thought and intention with love and trust to a higher place or power. When prayer is used for healing, it is the three nonphysical aspects, mental, emotional, and spiritual, that are being used to affect the physical. With all four aspects balanced by and connected to one another, how can they not affect one another?

Larry Dossey authored the books *Prayer is Good Medicine, Be Careful What You Pray For,* and *Reinventing Medicine.* In these books he shares documented studies regarding the power of prayer in healing. One such study by Drs. Krucoff and Crater was presented to a group of cardiologists at the American Heart Association's annual meeting in 1998. Their study was impressive because not only were the outcomes of the prayed-for group fifty to one hundred percent higher than those of the control group but also the prayer was done by members of a variety of religions, rather than one specific religious organization. Another study was done by Father Sean O'Laoire, a catholic priest. His double-blind study showed the same impressive results but with an interesting twist. Dr. O'Laoire discovered that *those doing the praying improved even more than those prayed for.*

When a person dies, there is still a body lying there. The spirit or the "animation" in the body is gone. The part of that person that was "life" is gone. The part that made that person unique is gone. You can *feel* that the person is gone, yet the physical body is still there. It is the spirit that is gone, the non-physical aspect of the individual's being. It was the spirit that made this individual the person he or she was. Why is it often difficult for us to understand this concept and embrace the spirit in each of us?

We are spiritual beings that have a physical experience.

Religion

Although some readers may expect us to discuss religion in this section on the nonphysical, we have chosen not to do so. We respect and hold in high regard the spiritual lessons of great teachers such as Jesus, Buddha, Mohammed, Moses, and

Jehovah. It is because of our respect for them that we have intentionally avoided the discussion of religion. We choose instead to explore broader-based spiritual concepts.

Stages of Spiritual Growth

Could it be that infants and young children are in a state of still being very much connected to spirit? Just what are babies looking at as they gaze into space, laugh, and wave? Perhaps they see more than we do. Have you ever wondered whether it is really true that many of the dying see angels, white light, and deceased loved ones moments before their own deaths? Perhaps it makes sense that never are we closer to that spiritual realm than when we first arrive in a physical body at birth and as we are preparing to depart at death.

Once we begin to develop our conscious minds and the traits of logic, rationale, judgment, and analysis, our focus usually shifts to the external world. Instead of the state of "being" we were in as children, we now come into a state of "doing." Goals are set, and accomplishments become the key to recognition and praise. Attention moves from inward spiritual attunement to outward personality directed positioning. Operating from this externally directed space generally lasts until somewhere around middle age. It is generally there that many begin to question the purpose of life. All the external parts of life may be in place just as worked and planned for, yet suddenly there is the realization that something is missing. All the "external stuff" hasn't made a happy person. We will often then look at our spouses, jobs, homes, possessions—all that makes up our lives—for clues as to what changes need to be made. We may look at what other or better things we need to have to make us happy. However, in the end it is entirely possible that nothing physical will be able to make us happy. What is really needed is to go inward and to get to know ourselves all over again, to open to our spirituality, our nonphysical nature.

As children we are born as free as butterflies. As adolescents and young adults we are often wrapped in a cocoon of physical illusion—only to break free again as butterflies when we acknowledge the spirit within. Like the butterfly leaving its cocoon, we are reborn when we are again awakened to the notion that we are spiritual beings. We can open our wings and fly when we realize that we are connected at a nonphysical level to all life. This life force is the energy that is the very basis of existence. If you believe in it, it does not matter what you call it.

Exercise 4-2: Am I happy?

Take a look at your life. Do you see the stages of growth as we have shown them? Where are you on this journey? Are you happy with your life at present?

Looking inward, are there any changes you want to make?

Empowerment and Truth

When we come to this place of moving into alignment with our spirit, we are becoming authentically empowered. This happens primarily from our feelings about ourselves. This power owes its strength to our commitment to ourselves and our *highest truth*. Our highest truth is what we know about ourselves, God, universal law, and life. It is at the core of our being and often is beyond belief or conjecture. Our truth resonates in us at a level of absolute knowingness, at a level so deep it is just something we know that we know. It is often undefinable and undefendable, and yet ultimately that does not matter because our personal truth is the source from which we express "who" we are.

When at the core of our beings we know our truth and act upon it, we are in a state of empowerment.

When we acknowledge that which feels right (our truth) and begin to honor it, we are honoring ourselves. Our truth becomes our comfort zone. *What we do when we honor ourselves is give ourselves permission to have our truth be the highest priority in our lives.* We can continue to embrace concepts and beliefs from family, church, and society as long as they are aligned to, and congruent with, our own personal truth.

As we know, children operate out of their subconscious minds and accept much of what they hear as fact. Most of us were taught what to say, think, and feel by our parents, teachers, religions, and society at large. Once we become reconnected to our highest truth, it is time to question our beliefs and perceptions and ask ourselves whether they are still true for us. Ask yourself, "Does this belief serve my greatest good?" If not, you can opt to change it so that it more accurately reflects the who and what you have become. When you do this, your highest truth becomes the barometer by which you gauge what comes into your life. When you continually use the question, "Is this true for me?" and when you honor your highest truth at the very core of your being and act upon it, you are living an empowered life.

Living our highest truth, living an empowered life, is never about power over anyone or anything. It is never about a feeling of superiority. It is a very personal journey, one that we live with integrity.

Living a personally empowered life is a reflection of our connection to "spirit" and is a life lived with integrity.

Benefits of Empowerment:

- Being authentic because we know who we are and what we stand for
- Gaining strength by coming from a place of integrity
- Improved relationships because we come from a clear, calm space
- Higher self-esteem and self-worth
- Improved communication by expressing our authentic selves
- Establishing priorities that genuinely reflect "who" we really are
- Learning to say "No," which creates more time for living our personal truth

Exercise 4-3: Your truth

Have you ever stopped to question your beliefs and perceptions? Are they really *true* for you or just programming you have received? What is your highest truth? Do you live in alignment with it? If not, what do you need to do differently?

How to Differentiate between Personality and Spirit

There is a difference between personality and spirit. They are both completely nonphysical aspects of self. In fact, combined, they make up the essence of "who" we are in this physical existence. One is pure truth. The other is a combination of all our beliefs and perceptions manifested outwardly by our behavior and actions. Our personal truth is in alignment with our spirit. Once we have become clear in recognizing our personal truth, we will find that living in our truth is a more comfortable place to be than the oftentimes more dramatic road traveled by our personalities. By recognizing our personal truth, we allow space for our personalities to change to reflect new behaviors and actions. This leads to a more spiritual life.

This journey of spirit is not about conquering the personality. It is not an internal war. It is about using our keen powers of observation and our deep desire to be whole and joyful. It allows us to see where our beliefs, perceptions, behaviors, and actions do not serve our highest good. Once recognized, these can become areas for healing and change.

A word of caution: we each need our personality in order to live effectively in this time, on this planet. Although our personalities may appear to encompass those qualities that seem to be negative, they have purpose. It is our having lived a more personality-controlled life that allows our understanding of these qualities. It also allows us to understand others who may still be primarily expressing characteristics of their personality.

Truly spiritual people have not tamed their personalities, but rather have blended it with their spirits.

Each of us is human. Life is a journey. Even when living in alignment with spirit, there will be times when we slip into negativity or feel out of balance. At these times, it can be difficult to see clearly. The checklist below can assist you in ascertaining whether you are coming from a place of the negative aspects of your personality or more purely from spirit.

Personality	Spirit
Fear and protection	Love
Limitation	Limitlessness
Attitude of separateness	Recognizes unity
Victim	Personal responsibility
Judgment	Accepts others
Pleasing others	Being genuine
Guilt and worry	Living in present moment

By stopping to look at where you really are, you can more clearly see the path that lies ahead. This path leads to healing. Do not judge yourself. These are opportunities for healing, and there will be many such opportunities on the road ahead. Think of life as a journey, rather than a necessity to reach a destination. The journey is the whole trip. Enjoy!

Do you have the perception that to live a spiritual life, you must be obviously religious like a nun, priest, or monk? Do you think living a spiritual life means you must live in such a way that *others* can *see* you are in worship and service to God? This is far from the truth. A spiritual person lives a life of integrity, in alignment with his or her highest truth. It is quiet and personal. Living a spiritual life allows us to view humanity as a whole. It does not separate us from other people, from other life forms on the planet, from the planet itself, or for that matter, from ourselves!

Spiritual Living Means:

- Living with integrity and purpose
- Getting in touch with our highest truth
- Releasing limitations
- Feeling the freedom of our individual spirits

- Honoring our commitments
- Feeling our connection to all life and forms of life
- Opening to receive abundance
- Expressing openly, honestly, and freely the uniqueness that is you

Manifestation

We now know that we create with thought and can manifest our life experiences through our thoughts, whatever they may be. Let's look at the process of manifesting with the intention of bringing something into being. In this way manifestation is the creation of an item, event, or experience by utilizing the principles associated with thought, emotion, intention, detachment, and faith. The four steps to manifestation are:

1. Clearly decide what it is you desire to bring into being.
2. Write it down and say it out loud, clearly and concisely.
3. Identify the feelings you want to experience when your desire is manifested.
4. Detach from the outcome and trust that the universe will take care of the details.

Look at each of these steps. First, you must know what it is you intend to manifest or create. Creatively visualize or bring to mind the details. If it is a car, what make, model, and year is it? What color and interior do you desire? Know it so clearly that you can see each detail in your mind's eye. If it is a new job, what will you be doing, with whom, at what hours, at what location, etc.? In this step the details are very important.

Second, state your intention and what you choose to manifest out loud. Even better, write all the details and then state them out loud. Sending your intention out into the universe verbally adds attention and support. It directs focused energy.

Third, identify the feelings you wish to experience. Often you will find it is the feelings that you most desire. How will you feel when you have the new car or new job? Are you searching for a sense of security, safety, happiness, or feeling fulfilled? What other emotions do you desire to feel? Know those feelings intimately. Imagine yourself already feeling that way.

And last, let go. The principles at work in manifestation are universal. It is necessary to *trust* in the principles and *know* that they work. This is your nonphysical reality at work here, just as you know when you turn on the television that there will be a picture or know when you answer your phone that someone will be there. When you use the principles of manifestation, *you put energy to work.* Then detach from the outcome and *know* that this, or something greater, will come to be. In fact, a good way to release your desire to the universe is to state, "This or something better is coming to me now for my greater good and the greatest good of all concerned." When you let go and trust, you are trusting in God and in universal law. You are trusting the universe to manifest that which is for your highest good and for all those concerned.

At times it may not seem as if your desire has manifested in the way you desired. Check to see whether it has manifested in some way other than the exact picture you had in mind. There may be those of you who are thinking, "Yeah right, I've wanted something real badly before and thought about it all the time, and I never got it." If this is true for you, think back: did you properly apply all the steps?

There is a difference between "wanting" and manifesting.

If you are in a place of wanting, you will be supported in your wanting, just as you will be supported in your manifesting.

You must move from the place of wanting (future tense) to the place of having (present tense). If you stay in the place of wanting, you stay in the future and the future never happens; *it is always in the future.* If you have not moved into the present, if you have not seen yourself having, then you have not created it in your life. This may be another reason that something you have tried to manifest in the past may not have appeared. Another may be, quite simply, that it was not for your greatest good at that time. Again, trust!

Manifesting uses many of the principles you have come to know and brings them together. By using thought, imagination, desire, intention, attention, emotion, and detachment, to name a few, you truly can create your reality. You really can "live the life you choose."

Full Circle

We now know that our world consists of nonphysical reality. Our thoughts, emotions, spirit, and even our physical bodies are really all nonphysical, ...just energy, consciousness, and empty space. If it feels as though we have come full circle, it's because we have.

In the beginning, all we were was energy, pure spirit, and as spirit, pure truth. Right now, in this physical existence, we have the opportunity to remember and to live in alignment with that truth. We each can let our highest truth be the source of who we are. Living our truth creates honor, honesty, and integrity.

Take a moment to really ponder this wondrous information. How simple yet how complex life really is. Pause and reflect on how you have set up your priorities. The exercise below will show you what those priorities are and what you love most in your life.

Exercise 4-4: What are your priorities?

Imagine that for the next six months you have all the money you want, perfect health, and no need to work. You can do anything and have anything you want. Then at the end of six months you are going to die a peaceful death. What would you do in this time period? What would be your priorities? Write them down.

Now look at your choices. Did you find your priorities were about people, things, career, nature? Take time to put your priorities in perspective and to reflect on them. Are you living them now? Are your intentions receiving your attention? If not, why? Try this if you find yourself getting caught up in the conflicts and petty concerns in your daily life. Ask yourself, "In the grand scheme of things is *this* really that big a deal?" Looking at the big picture often helps put life in perspective.

Section Four Highlights:

- The very essence of physical reality is that it is essentially nonphysical.
- "Modern" technology is based on the nonphysical.
- The nonphysical aspect of life is spirit.
- We are spiritual beings that have a physical experience.
- Our spirit is our life force and is connected to the universal life force.
- As children we begin life more connected to our spirituality. At some point our focus shifts to external growth and success.
- Authentic empowerment comes from living our highest truth.
- Our spirits are pure truth while our personalities are a combination of all our beliefs and perceptions manifested outwardly by our behavior and actions.
- We are in balance and harmony when we blend our personalities with our spirits.
- Manifestation is the power of creation working in our lives.
- *Everything is nonphysical!*

Afterword

We hope that you have enjoyed this book, but more important we hope that you have learned about yourself, your life, and your potential. We hope that you have found your truth.

We have searched for our truth in the process of living our own individual lives. Through books, classes, and teachers we have been exposed over and over to someone else's truth. Through this, we have discovered our own. This book is *our* truth. Our goal in writing this book has been to share our truth with you in the hopes that it will help you discover, or begin to discover, your own. With this book, or any other, the key is to sift through what the teaching brings and to see what fits for you. What "feels" right? That, as you now know, is your truth! Congratulations! This is the key to unlocking your potential! *Know your truth!* Use it to measure everything in your world!

If, while reading this book, you found yourself frustrated that we did not go into more depth about a certain concept, note that as a good place to start your own individual search for truth. Our goal was to introduce concepts. Our goal was to leave you hungry. Our greatest desire in writing this book was that you would continue from this point on to seek answers, to learn, and to grow. A good place to start is with the books on the Recommended Reading list.

Enjoy your journey!

Recommended Reading

**Most authors listed below have published many books.
We have listed our favorites.**

Deepak Chopra	*Seven Spiritual Laws of Success* and *Quantum Healing*
Gary Zukav	*Seat of the Soul*
Marianne Williamson	*A Return to Love*
Caroline Myss	*Anatomy of the Spirit* and *Energy Anatomy* (audio)
Candace Pert, Ph.D.	*Molecules of Emotion*
Wayne Dyer	*You Will See It When You Believe It*
Shakti Gawain	*Living in the Light*
Jerry Fankhauser	*The Power of Affirmations*
Don Miguel Ruiz	*The Four Agreements*
Louise Hay	*You Can Heal Your Life*
Bruce Lipton, Ph.D.	*The Biology of Perception/Psychology of Change* (video tape)
Phil McGraw	*Self Matters*
Betty Bethards	*The Dream Book*
Larry Dossey	*Reinventing Medicine*

Written in story form:

James Redfield	*The Celestine Prophesy*
Brian Weiss, M.D.	*Many Lives, Many Masters*
Richard Bach	*Illusions*
Marlo Morgan	*Mutant Message*
Betty Eadie	*Embraced by the Light*

ORDER FORM

Would you like to order additional copies of *The Key to Me* for friends and family? Copies are available from the publisher.

☐ To order by mail complete this order form and mail it with your check or money order to:

Spiderweb Publishing
136 W. Hlavka
Maple City, MI 49664

☐ To order by credit card visit theWeb site:
www.LiveTrue.com

Name:_____

Address: _____

City:_____ State: _____ Zip: _____

Phone: _____ E-mail: _____

Credit Card #: _____ Exp. Date: _____

Signature: _____

Please send me ___copies @ $12.95/ea. $ _____

(Discounts are available on orders of   MI tax (6%) $ _____
four or more. Contact us for details.)   Postage & Handling $ ___$3.50_____

                                      Total $ _____

Spiderweb Publishing
136 W. Hlavka
Maple City, MI 49664
(231) 228-6839
www.LiveTrue.com

Cathleen Follansbee, C.Ht., is a professional healing practitioner with private practices in northwestern lower Michigan and Los Angeles, Calif. Her healing technique blends her expertise as a Reiki Master, Transformational Breath Specialist, and Hypnotherapist with the pure energy work of Esoteric Healing and Chinese Energetic Medicine. She is a corporate officer and business administrator of Traverse Tops Inc., founder of LiveTrue.com, and cofounder of Spiderweb Publishing. She is an avid writer and has published several articles. In her California practice, Cathy works regularly with film and theater artists.

Cathy has lived in Leelanau County, Mich., since 1980, where she balances a busy schedule with her passion for her family and friends. *The Key to Me* is her first book.

Russell LeBlanc, D.C., graduated Magna Cum Laude from Life Chiropractic College in 1981. While at Life College, he was class president and a member of the Pi Tau Delta Fraternity. Dr. Russ is a diplomate of the National Board of Chiropractic Examiners and a member of the Michigan Chiropractic Society. He has served on the Board of Directors for the Georgia Chiropractic Counsel and the Leelanau Children's Center. Russ enjoys public speaking and often teaches life success principles to school and civic groups.

Presently, Dr. Russ and his wife have a large chiropractic family practice in northern Michigan. He is interested in integrative health care and serves on the Board of Directors for Leelanau Memorial Health Center and on the Corporate Board of Munson Medical Center.

*To contact the authors and for information regarding their workshops and seminars, visit the Website **www.LiveTrue.com***

Author Biographies